The Other Couch

Discovering Women's Wisdom in Therapy

Patricia Peters Martin, Ph.D.
Helene DeMontreux Houston, M.S., APRN

What People Are Saying

With great compassion, wisdom, and grace, Patricia and Helene help us understand the profound and intimate bond between client and therapist. Like the very best of educators who foster two-way conversations to guide teaching and learning, they explore the process of discovery that results in the ultimate triumph of a relationship. The client and the therapist learn from each other. The stories revealed in *The Other Couch* find their way into our hearts and, as promised, will enrich and heal our worlds.

—Carol A. Leary, Ph.D.
President, Bay Path University, Longmeadow, Massachusetts

A wonderful book. The authors present a collection of extraordinarily varied and real stories of women in therapy. Here the insights come not so much from the therapists, but from the clients themselves. Their wisdom is touching and powerful.

—Anthony E. Wolf, Ph.D.
Practicing psychologist and author of six parenting books including,
Get Out of My Life, but First Could You Drive Me and Cheryl to the Mall?
A Parent's Guide to the New Teenager

Storytelling at its best! Through the eyes and ears of their therapists, 36 women share their intimate stories of vulnerability and of ultimate power. With sensitivity and empathy these wise women, both therapists and clients, inspire us to find our inner strength and to choose healing.

—Mary Reap, IHM, Ph.D.
President, Elms College, Chicopee, Massachusetts

Take a seat on *The Other Couch: Discovering Women's Wisdom in Therapy* and be reminded that, whatever your challenge or situation, others have walked similar paths—and survived to tell the tale of transformation. Big thanks to all the women who consented to have their stories told on these pages, and to Patricia Peters Martin and Helene De Montreux Houston for the difference they've made to those patients and the possibilities they put forth to the lucky readers of this book.

—Suzanne Strempek Shea
author of 11 novels and her most recent publication,
This Is Paradise: An Irish Mother's Grief, an African Village's Plight,
and the Medical Clinic That Brought Fresh Hope to Both.

This inspirational book by Dr. Patricia Martin and Helene Houston gives us insight into the lives of women who teach us about courage, conviction and deep faith. These stories will make you laugh and cry as you turn page after page to experience the lives of these ordinary, but extraordinary, women.

—Mary McGeer, SSJ
Pastoral Associate, St. Michael's Church,
East Longmeadow, MA and author of
I've Kept a Memory of You All This Time.

NorLightsPress.com
762 State Road 458
Bedford, IN 47421

Printed in the United States of America
ISBN:978-0-9964559-1-6

Edited by Sammie Justesen
Cover Design by Vorris Justesen
Book Design by Nadene Carter
Photography by Erin Chrusciel

First printing, 2015

Dedication

To the women who have permitted us to write their stories, as well as
the many other women who have been our patients
and impacted our lives.

Contents

Stories of Loss

Having Children

Serious Illness

Final Words

Our Stories

Acknowledgements

IT WAS QUITE AN exhilarating "woohoo" moment when we sent our final edited manuscript to the publisher. We've had quite a journey together writing this book. Helene and I have become dear friends and supported each other through many uphill climbs and downhill thrilling rides. So first and foremost, thank you to my writing buddy!

Next on the list of people to acknowledge are our steadfast editor and publishers, Sammie and Dee Justesen and Nadene Carter. We feel so fortunate to have found NorLightsPress and thank our lucky stars (pun intended) to have such wonderful guidance along the way.

For, Patricia, who originates from Indiana it was a journey home to the rolling hills of Brown County. For Helene it was a new adventure. We had such fun designing and redesigning our book cover. We joke that emails that go into cyberspace are riding on a magic carpet with a red apple. (The carpet and red apple are on the editing floor from former cover design prospects).

We are grateful to all the women who so willingly and eagerly allowed us to write their stories in this book. The overwhelming response of "YES," was often followed by "I think my story will help someone else." We truly appreciate their generosity of spirit. Also, sincere thanks to all the many clients we've had the pleasure to work with during our seventy-plus combined years of practicing psychotherapy. Every client had a story to tell and could have been included in this book. We believe that, in many ways, each of them is part of the stories we present. We have grown in wisdom and compassion thanks to all of you.

We have been permitted to utilize the words of women poets in our book. We thank Margot Eckert for her insightful Foreword and poem, "My Therapist." You will find Barbara Ardinger's wonderful poem "There is a Web of Women" in the chapter on finding your sisters. She can be reached at www.barbaraardinger.com and on her website on Feminism and Religion http://feminismandreligion.com. Danna Faulds wrote the beautiful poem at the end of the narratives, "The Open Door" which can be found on page 32 of *From Root to Bloom: Yoga Poems and Other Writings*. (Morris Publishing, 2006).

To our wonderful husbands and families, we express deep love and appreciation for your support as we typed away at our computers over many days and nights. The moniker of Computer Girls became our nicknames during the months of editing and revisions. We both are fortunate to have such kind, dear husbands. Together, may we walk many more roads and share life's journey.

To our grown children who have offered technical advice and suggestions on the title and cover design, and who were fabulous cheerleaders, we say, "Thank you and we love you!"

And finally, we wish to thank all the wonderful authors, both fiction and non-fiction who have spun compelling stories that illuminate and capture the human spirit and make the world a more positive place. The success of narrative medicine—using the psychological and personal history of the patient to help educate new medical providers and prevent them from losing their humanity—is a testament to the power of story.

Foreword

CALLING A THERAPIST is a huge step in one's life. Therapy takes time and money, two things in especially short supply when life becomes complicated and awful. Time and money are the first two obstacles we overcome.

The third barrier to therapy is even more challenging: Saying, "I need help!" This statement seems to encompass many things: failure, incompetence, weakness, mistakes, and character flaws—all unpleasant thoughts that add to your misery. With three good reasons not to make an appointment, you may decide to continue telling yourself: "I can do this alone."

But sometimes we can't manage by ourselves. If you feel this way, *The Other Couch* is a good book for you. The stories in this book dispel the notion of the therapist as an intimidating, judgmental wizard behind the curtain in Oz. Having gone through therapy myself, I know the process is more like consulting an urban planner who helps you lay down a street design, add traffic lights and entertainment areas, and makes sure you include plenty of green parkland in your vision.

By making that first appointment, you acknowledge the need for assistance. Who doesn't need help prioritizing decisions, sorting out confusion, and filtering the voices inside our heads?

What of the therapist? *The Other Couch* speaks to the reciprocity in the room despite all the degrees on the wall. First, you are important enough to be helped. Second, the therapist is your helper—providing swimming lessons for some and a life preserver for others. You will still do the heavy work to get to a better place. And as you figure it out, and when you're headed down a path that feels right, you will know when the time comes to walk on your own.

This book is filled with the wisdom of many women who are walking on their better paths with the help of skilled therapists like Dr. Patricia Martin and Helene

Houston, and who are happy to celebrate the changes in their lives. Knowing that each patient's journey makes the therapist a better counselor and wiser for having known this person shows us that therapy is, indeed, a two-way path.

Margot Eckert, J.D.
Secondary School Educator
Former patient of Dr. Patricia Peters Martin

My Therapist

You give a name to my feelings.
You let me cry.
I flit from topic to pain.
Can I give you this much awfulness?
"What else happened?" you say.
I read, watch, and listen to the news each day.
"What is *your* news?" you ask.
"What is your current event?"
This, that, and this. What is happening to me, I ask?
Am I losing my mind? I am scared of tomorrow.
"You are on a current." you say.
When will it end?
"I don't know," you say, "But it will end."
You name the pain. You sponge the pain.
You guide the boat through fierce white water.
"You can cry," you say. "It is good to cry.
Tears take your river to a new place."

—Margot Eckert
Copyright @ February 8, 2015

Introduction

THIS IS A BOOK about the wisdom of women; specifically women who sought therapy, entered our offices as patients, and left our practices as our teachers. These are stories of struggle and healing.

The Other Couch: Discovering Women's Wisdom in Therapy reveals the remarkable lives of 36 women. As a clinical psychologist (Patricia) and a clinical nurse specialist (Helene), we felt prompted to tell the stories of women who've touched our hearts and lives during our combined years of doing psychotherapy.

The Other Couch celebrates women we've known and learned from over the years. These women taught us courage, patience, acceptance, and how to live a good life. It's no coincidence that the derivation of "inspire" in Latin (inspirare), not only means "in spirit" but also "breath." The ability to learn to breathe and live life fully, breath by breath, is something we learned from these women during our time together in therapy. These are women who struggled and survived through grit and determination; women, who are willing to share their unique, yet universal stories with other women who pick up this book.

These stories are meant to inspire because they bring new life, breath, and spirit into the world. *The Other Couch* is a tribute to courageous women everywhere. This book is different from other therapy discussion books because we focus on the knowledge and wisdom patients bring to their therapists rather than discussing the advice mental health workers give their clients.

As seasoned therapists we've reached the stage in our lives where we want to make a difference—to write, teach, and share what we've learned. For most women this stage of life begins after the age of 50, when we're done with nurturing and childbearing. In the fifth and sixth decades of life we enter a new phase of creativity and self-expression. And, if we're fortunate, we have time to integrate, reflect, and understand the earlier part of our lives.

The intended book audience is women, particularly women in their 40's through 70's—the largest reading population. Anna Quindlen, the female story teller of our generation, praises the virtues of aging in her current book, *Lots of Candles, Plenty of Cake.*[1]

Many of us have come to a surprising conclusion about this moment of our lives. It's that we've done a pretty good job of becoming ourselves, and that this is, in so many ways, the time of our lives. As Carly Simon once sang, "These are the good old days." Lots of candles, plenty of cake. I wouldn't be twenty-five again on a bet, or even forty. And when I say this to other women at lunch, everyone around the table nods. Many of us find ourselves exhilarated, galvanized, at the very least older and wiser.

Like Anna Quindlen, we believe each life story is precious and deserves to be told and heard. We feel honored by the stories we've heard and the wise people we've met during our years of doing psychotherapy. We believe every human being is capable of change and growth, sometimes through unbearable circumstances. In this spirit, we present the stories of women who've shared their most personal and intimate details with us.

In these pages you'll meet Lori, who struggled with childhood sexual abuse and adult alcoholism and is now accomplishing great things as a school administrator.

You'll read sage advice from a 92 year old woman who entered therapy after her 87 year old brother died.

You will be introduced to Leslie, who successfully maneuvered the devastating diagnosis of leukemia in her nine year old son and now shares her coping strategies.

You'll meet Delores, who courageously survived the death of her beloved husband of fifty-four years.

In *The Other Couch*, we want to talk about life as though we're sitting down over a cup of coffee to share our joys and sorrows, obstacles and passageways. You will be privy to the patients' point of view and the therapists' point of view as we narrate the journeys of these inspiring women. We hope these stories will humanize therapists and provide a window into the therapy process, while also respecting and valuing the stories of our patients.

We have changed identities and obtained permission from the clients to use their stories. Occasionally the narratives have been altered and fictionalized to protect the identities of our patients and enhance the narrative.

---

1   Anna Quindlen, *Lots of Candles, Plenty of Cake*, Random House, 2013.

In our busy culture, too many people's stories are only heard by their psychotherapists. We're surrounded by self-centeredness, violence, addiction, stress, and many other negative forces. It's time to read stories that will enrich and heal our worlds. In writing this book, we pass on this wisdom to you—the wisdom of everyday women who have opened their hearts and lives to us. May this book be a meaningful story for you.

Patricia Peters Martin, Ph.D.
Helene DeMontreux Houston, M.S., APRN

Relationships

Chapter 1
The Cheating Spouse:
Do I Really Need to Forgive Him?

Patricia

MANY PEOPLE COME to therapy angry and hurt—with feelings directly related to abuse suffered at the hands of a spouse. Cruelty may take the form of physical abuse, verbal and emotional abuse, sexual abuse, or a combination of the above. Once a patient is able to verbalize her emotional pain and begin healing, the next step is forgiveness, right?

Maybe not. For many people forgiveness seems like a lie and causes even more harm and pain.

Such was the case with my client Cynthia, a classic looking fifty-something woman with high cheekbones and an elegant appearance, even when she wore a plain shirt and pants. At our first meeting Cynthia looked like a tired, worn out person who'd experienced much sadness. As her story unfolded I understood her fatigue and mournful demeanor.

Cynthia originally came to therapy to see if she could bear staying in a relationship with Frank, her husband, who'd recently returned from a trip and curtly informed her, "You'd better get to a doctor and be checked for gonorrhea."

He went on to explain that he'd been with prostitutes and contracted the sexually transmitted disease. Cynthia was appalled, but not totally shocked. She knew he'd been unfaithful in the past with office interns and other women.

When I asked why she stayed with him, she responded flatly, "I always try to forgive."

When I inquired how that had worked so far, she replied, "I actually have a lot of trouble with forgiveness."

No wonder, I thought.

As I came to more fully understand Cynthia over multiple sessions, I realized she was a bright, insightful, philosophical woman, and truly committed to living as a good Christian. She felt forgiving was the right thing to do, but it was next to impossible with her husband. In their marriage, Cynthia's forgiveness began to feel like a revolving door policy. As fast as she forgave Frank one infidelity, he committed another. She realized that although she admired certain things about her husband—his wit, his intellect, his wild and wonderful playful side—she hated the lies, cheating, and cruelty. He would shower her with affection and want to make passionate love one week, only to turn on her the next week with spiteful criticism and put downs. He verbally assaulted her with a barrage of insults. He seemed to hate everything about her, from how she cooked to how she decorated. He made comments like, "You cook such damn awful food and it's disgusting to watch you eat. I hate how you dress and you embarrass me in public. You are such a %#&% disappointment as a wife."

While Cynthia struggled with guilt at not being a desirable wife and homemaker, Frank continued doing whatever he wanted, with no remorse. He managed to blame Cynthia for his infidelities by telling himself she wasn't a good wife and he deserved better.

She grieved the loss of the marriage she'd hoped for when she said "I do," twenty-eight years earlier. She felt increasingly angry and bitter with Frank and thought about leaving him, but wondered how she'd support herself and the one child who still lived at home.

The last straw finally came for Cynthia just before a weekend they planned as a romantic getaway. Her bags were already packed, including new lingerie she bought just for him, when Frank announced he'd made other plans. He added, "Why would anyone want to go on vacation with you?"

Cynthia felt like a bolt of lightning had struck her. Without thinking, she shouted, "Get the hell out of here! I don't want you in my life anymore!"

Frank was ready to leave and moved out that night.

Finally, Cynthia had enough. She went to a lawyer the next day and obtained a temporary order for Frank to pay the mortgage and provide child support. Then she filed for divorce, which was granted, plus a surprise decree by the judge for "cruel and abusive treatment." This was a vindication of sorts for Cynthia. She since went on to have the marriage annulled by the Catholic Church.

But the forgiveness factor was still a big issue, because Cynthia believed she needed to forgive her ex-husband and "move on." Members of her church and popular literature extolled the virtues of forgiveness, but she wrestled with the idea of forgiving such atrocities. To forgive seemed like condoning her ex's behavior and she could not in good conscience do so. I often told Cynthia she didn't need to forgive, but she did need to release the baggage of this relationship and try to let go. I understood her dilemma, as I've had situations in my own life that were difficult to forgive.

I believe forgiveness isn't always possible, especially when the offender isn't sorry and doesn't admit he did anything wrong. I searched for books to help Cynthia understand how it's possible to move on without forgiving.

The book that gave Cynthia her Eureka moment was, *How Can I Forgive You? The Courage to Forgive, the Freedom Not To*, by Janis Abrahms Spring, Ph. D.[2] In this breakthrough book, Spring describes six critical tasks for earning forgiveness. I like the word earning, because I believe it's the perpetrator's responsibility to EARN forgiveness. Tasks for the perpetrator are:

1. Look at your mistaken assumptions of forgiveness.
2. Bear witness to the pain you caused.
3. Apologize genuinely, responsibly, and non-defensively.
4. Seek to understand your behavior and reveal the inglorious truth about yourself to the person you harmed.
5. Work to earn back trust.
6. Forgive yourself for injuring another person.

Clearly, Cynthia's ex had done none of the above. After reading Spring's book she felt relieved and spiritually lighter. She was absolved from having to forgive and no longer needed to carry that burden.

Many of the above steps for earning forgiveness remind me of the Twelve Step program in Alcoholics Anonymous, which involves the alcoholic taking a self-inventory and ultimately making amends to people who were harmed. The theory is, an addict cannot find serenity and healing without admitting what he or she has done to others and asking forgiveness. Cynthia's husband Frank isn't an alcoholic, but clearly has sexual addictions. Because of Frank's self-centeredness and narcissism I sincerely doubt he will ever take the step of making amends to anyone, especially to Cynthia.

Now Cynthia is moving on one day at a time to rebuild her life and self-worth. An adequate financial settlement from the divorce allowed her to stay in her home. She cut off all contact with Frank and her three grown children want nothing to do with their philandering father. Part of her rebuilding is literal. She's making household repairs that were long neglected, something Frank refused to do. (Did I mention he was also a cheapskate?) The first thing she accomplished with her home was symbolic—she had the sagging foundation shored up. She got rid of clutter, installed insulated windows, and began painting and redecorating to please her own taste.

---

2   Spring, Janice Abrahms, *How Can I Forgive You? The Courage to Forgive, The Freedom Not To*, (New York: William Morrow Publisher), February, 2005, p. 126.

Cynthia also attends my monthly support group for women in abusive relationships. I discovered she's a wonderful resource for younger women who need help leaving abusive situations. In our group she nurtures and pilots others. She also volunteers with a group of Catholic nuns who focus on the issue of human trafficking.

And finally, Cynthia has learned it is her choice to forgive or not to forgive. This poem she wrote describes her struggles as an abused wife.

I Am a Window

I am a window painted shut.
Your shouting grimes my glass.
Your lies smear my glass.
Your shoving cracks my glass.
My cold glass pane still shields me from your painful rocks,
while I look far outside for a way to get out.
But for now
I am a window painted shut.

Resources:

www.aa.org
www.12step.org

Research: McNulty, J.K. "The dark side of forgiveness: The tendency to forgive predicts continued psychological and physical aggression in marriage," *Personality and Social Psychology Bulletin*, 2011, 37, p.770-783.

Author's note: Although many studies describe the positive effects of forgiveness, until recently scholars hadn't examined the negative implications of forgiving—including the idea that forgiveness gives offenders a free pass from responsibility for their actions. McNulty's study found that, once forgiven, offenders don't have to face anger, criticism, rejection, or loneliness that might discourage them from reoffending. McNulty's report and others, show that: "Forgiveness of infidelity leads to more infidelity. Forgiveness is saying, 'It's okay,' which may just be the fuel a transgressing spouse needs for more lapses in judgment."

Chapter 2
Separation Anxiety: I Can't Say Goodbye

Helene

TERRY'S GYNECOLOGIST FIRST referred her to me. She was the ultimate PMS woman, suffering from dramatic mood swings punctuated by bursts of rage, recurrent depression, and severe anxiety. Terry always felt remorse after she lost control of her emotions and she felt especially uncomfortable with the rage that simmered within her.

Throughout our work together when I pointed out her rage Terry became defensive and even angry. Her body and face would stiffen and her gaze changed, with her eyes turning cold and looking past me. I saw that expression many times in our work together. When this change happened, I never pointed it out, but told myself, "I've hit a nerve." I knew I'd punctured the characteristic denial she displayed.

Terry is a beautiful young woman with large, penetrating blue eyes, glossy hair that sometimes covers half her face, and an engaging, wistful smile. Although she looked attractive, she agonized over periodic weight gains that destroyed her self-esteem. Struggling to diet and control her weight added to her overall stress.

Terry's emotional turmoil didn't prevent her from being an attentive parent to two small children, a devoted daughter to her parents, and a successful professional in a highly stressful and competitive job. I admired her ability to function at such a high level despite the terrible and hurtful distractions.

As Terry told her story during our first visit, I could see that her moods reflected her troubled marriage to Larry. He was a divorced man working as a successful salesman, and the job included frequent travel away from home. Besides that issue, he was developing a significant drinking problem that led to a DUI. Handsome and charming, he had many opportunities for cheating on the road—and Terry suspected he was unfaithful. While he was away and the cheating stayed hidden, she could play ostrich and go about her life.

But when Larry started an affair with a neighbor's wife the reality of the situation crashed in on Terry. The story came out and she felt enraged and humiliated to have his womanizing ways aired in public to friends and neighbors. She insisted on couple's counseling and during the sessions she discovered Larry was a serial philanderer, a sex addict. Things were even worse than she suspected.

Terry agonized over getting divorced, fully knowing life as a single mom wouldn't be easy. She had to commute a long way to her managerial job, plus she worried about the children's many extracurricular activities. She stressed over destroying their relationship with their father which was surprisingly good. To make matters worse, Larry's career floundered and he lost his job. Then she obsessively worried about the situation and had difficulty making a final decision. Antidepressants and antianxiety medications helped manage her PMS, mood swings, depression, and anxiety, but the enormity of the situation still weighed heavily on her.

After months of agonizing, Terry filed for divorce. She found it impossible to live in the neighborhood that held her greatest humiliation and was still home to the other woman. She and her children moved to a smaller, affordable home in the same community, at a comfortable distance from the old neighborhood. Life was better, but Terry still had difficulty setting limits for Larry who began treating her new home like his own. He would show up at dinner time and sometimes sleep over on the couch. Asking him to leave seemed cruel to her because he helped a lot with the children and drove them to their activities. She said the kids were much happier having him around.

During our sessions, Terry admitted to life-long difficulty with change and endings. I found myself feeling impatient when she seemed to slide back into her old behavior with Larry. I asked her if anything had changed. What had changed, she assured me, was her ability to establish firm boundaries on intimate contact. She made it clear to Larry those days were over. He did maintain an apartment, but Terry no longer worried if he was with someone else.

Gradually the two of them evolved a comfortable arrangement, with Larry remaining an involved, caring father. While Terry sometimes felt conflict about the arrangement, her rage toward Larry diminished. He would meet the children after school, drive them to their activities, and often had dinner with the family. The children seemed content with that arrangement and did well in school and sports. In therapy, Terry identified self-esteem and relationship issues that made decision making and endings so difficult for her. Her own parents had divorced and she grew up with much turmoil in her life.

Terry gradually seemed less guarded when telling me Larry was still in her life. They weren't married, but managed to have a different kind of family, centered around the children. It wasn't perfect or conventional, but it worked for them.

This unique arrangement helped me learn a lesson of suspending judgment. Sometimes an arrangement that seems so wrong can be exactly right.

Chapter 3
Codependency: The Last Straw
Helene

CO-DEPENDENT RELATIONSHIPS often lead to great emotional turmoil in the lives of therapy clients. Sometimes it takes patience for the therapist to recognize small, positive changes in these destructive relationships. We tend to hope for more significant results in our work with patients, and we may underestimate the power of a seemingly small change.

In a codependent relationship, a "caretaker" sacrifices his or her needs to take care of another person, often shutting down normal emotional responses. This self-sacrificing behavior may disguise an underlying need to control the other person or the situation. The caretaker's obsessiveness can mirror the addictive behavior of the person who's identified as the problem. Codependent wives of cheating sex addicts morph into private investigators, preoccupied with looking for incriminating emails, text messages, phone messages, and other clues. Mothers of addicts have similar preoccupations as they search for drug paraphernalia. Children of alcoholics learn to observe the subtlest signals to predict what their parent's behavior will be like. In Frank McCourt's *Angela's Ashes*,[3] the tilt of his father's cap forecast violence to come.

Codependent behaviors are learned behavior and may reflect growing up in an alcoholic or highly dysfunctional home where one person felt responsible for keeping the family on an even keel. These are the homes of "parentified children" who are given and accept responsibility and worry that goes far beyond their ages. These are the children who grow up with anxiety disorders and the need to have control in their lives—including control over their loved ones.

---

3   McCourt, Frank. *Angela's Ashes: A Memoir*. Scribner, May 25, 1999.

One day my client Betty rushed into a codependency group meeting looking stressed, her face pinched with worry. The other women had already discussed their concerns, so Betty launched into her news with, "I could be better." With her classic straight-faced, expressionless delivery, she reported dramatic events from the past month.

I've known Betty for 15 years. She entered treatment for a severe panic disorder and initially focused her concerns on her younger son, Steve. Unlike his older brother, Steve struggled in school and, beginning at age 13, had severe conflicts with his father. This made Betty sad, resentful of her husband, and protective of her son. She found herself defending Steve and making excuses for his increasingly irresponsible behavior. Gradually, as we got to know each other, Betty revealed that her husband, Gary (a medical professional) became controlling toward her early in their marriage. Among other things, he was sexually demanding and insisted she wear revealing clothes that made her uncomfortable.

Betty cared for their home and children along with working at a responsible job in a corporate office. In spite of all her contributions, Gary became more critical and verbally abusive over the years. Betty's self-esteem suffered and part of her believed she was always at fault, no matter what. In therapy I worked at trying to help her recognize that Gary's demands and accusations were inappropriate and downright wrong. But any headway we made was quickly lost at the next session when Betty presented another litany of alleged transgressions and damaged self-esteem. She probably was the most "stuck" of all the patients I've treated. I felt like the proverbial broken record and the term "beating a dead horse" took on new meaning.

After several years of individual treatment and medication management, I suggested Betty attend a codependency group I was co-leading. I hoped interacting with other women would help her identify the patterns in her behavior and interrupt the cycle of abuse. After more months of treatment she was able to identify her fear of being alone as the reason she couldn't move forward with separation or divorce. Her sensitivity to criticism seemed to develop in response to a highly critical and demanding mother who insisted on daily attention from Betty, even in Betty's adulthood. Women supposedly marry their fathers, but in this case Betty's father was a gentle soul. However, Betty's husband Gary was the mirror image of her difficult mother. Betty was so beaten down by the people in her life that her self-confidence had shattered, feeding her fear that she could never take care of herself.

To make matters worse, Gary refused couple's counseling and went on disability for a work related back injury. He spent thousands of dollars they couldn't afford on toys and hobbies. With Gary around the house all day, Betty no longer felt her home was her own. He drained their retirement account and bullied her to cosign for loans. She was not allowed to criticize his behavior and any comment led to vicious fights, followed by silence that unnerved her. His silent treatment left her feeling trapped in a state of anxiety in which she replayed the argument over and over, while her husband was perfectly happy pursuing his hobbies, including an online infatuation with another woman.

Meanwhile, their son Steve grew up irresponsible and had two children with a young woman who wouldn't marry him. Betty became involved in the lives of Steve, his girlfriend, and their children. The presence of vulnerable children kept Betty from establishing the boundaries that would help her untangle from codependent behavior. She spent thousands of dollars bailing Steve out of jail after increasingly serious scrapes with the law. She paid his fines for various offenses related to driving, drug use, and ultimately criminal behavior. Steve would promise to get work and repay the debts, but never followed through. He lived with Betty and Gary on and off, adding to the contentious atmosphere. Violence flared at times. Steve would behave like an out of control adolescent, whining for gas money and becoming verbally abusive and threatening (much like his father) when his mother had no money to give him. This dysfunctional cycle continued for years.

Meanwhile, in group therapy, the other women would sit expressionless as Betty recounted the mistreatment she felt from her husband, son, and mother. These were all events they'd heard before and their efforts to offer advice always fell on deaf ears. I ran out of suggestions and interventions and became acquainted with the term *vicarious traumatization*—when a therapist begins feeling helpless and defeated through a patient's traumas.

That special day in our codependency group meeting, Betty announced something had finally changed in her life during the past month. Gary had threatened divorce in the past, but never acted on it. Betty reported that, a few weeks earlier he took off his wedding ring and stopped wearing it. She said, "Something changed in me just like that. I no longer had feelings for him. He can be my friend, we can do things together, but I have no wish to be close to him."

The members of the group looked amazed; I struggled not to scream, "Hallelujah!"

As Betty continued her story, we learned that something also changed in Betty's attitude toward Steve. She found out he had a $400.00 a day drug habit. While she and Gary were out of town the week before, Steve and his felonious cousins stole thousands of dollars of equipment from their locked shed. He initially lied about his part in the theft, and then put his hand out for gas money. Betty told us she spent the next day pressing charges against her son for theft and insisting that a section 35 be enacted (commitment to a detox facility followed by rehab.)

She understood jail time might be involved—something he had barely avoided countless times before, thanks to her intervention. This time Betty described her intelligent, organized efforts with no tears and an obvious sense of relief. She began to focus on her own friends and interests. She had no intention of moving from her home. She said Gary's removal of his wedding ring and Steve's bald faced thievery and lies "were the last straw." The group of women who'd all suffered with addicted children nearly jumped for joy. This was truly a high five moment for all of us.

"The last straw" describes a pivotal event that triggers dramatic change in a person. Sadly it's often used to explain the cause of suicide or murder. But the last straw may also relate to something that catalyzes a breakthrough for a person stuck with unhealthy relationships. Sometimes last straws are less serious than the things Betty experienced with Steve.

When emotions have built up for years, even a simple comment or action can tip the scales and change everything. Whatever it is, the final straw in a pattern of behavior that's destructive to another person's self-worth becomes a tipping point that may lead to change.

The codependent behavior probably isn't over for Betty, and no doubt I'll be called on again to be patient with my client. Paradoxically, codependent people often show too much patience with those around them. Giving one more chance, bailing out, hiring the lawyer, paying the fees, lying to employers, caring for the children, and sacrificing financially are not the keys to changing a loved one's behavior. However, I have no intention of giving up on Betty!

Chapter 4
Stopping Abuse: It Wasn't the Frying Pan
Helene

I MET MATILDA about fifteen years ago when she was referred to a woman's group I was facilitating. She had just been discharged from the partial hospitalization program following an inpatient psychiatric admission. Her depression was so severe she had been totally shut down and at times out of touch with reality. She had been recovering from major surgery to treat colon cancer that had nearly killed her. Matilda suffered with a chronic depression that until now was untreated. A life that was filled with disappointments, loss, and domestic abuse fueled alcoholism she had overcome fifteen years earlier. A dramatic event stopped the physical abuse years ago, but her husband Leon's nasty temperament continued to wear on her self-esteem. Gradually as Matilda opened up in the group, she shared the stories of ending the drinking, ending the physical violence, and finding God.

Matilda is now in her seventies—a strikingly elegant African-American woman of generally few words. She is the sort of person who brings to mind the television commercial: "When E.F. Hutton speaks, people listen." In the group, when Matilda spoke, we all took notice because what she said was grounded in wisdom garnered from a life rich with experiences of hardship and survival.

Matilda met her current husband in 1965 in a small Northeastern city. Her first husband was a "no account" who didn't work. Her second husband, Leon, introduced her to alcohol when she was twenty. Leon was from the South, where, Matilda says, "wives were treated like children." His physical, verbal and emotional abuse started early on. "I guess I was like my Dad—I always tried to get away from a situation. I never wanted to fight." She describes her parents lovingly. "They never argued or fought; my Dad knew when to walk away from conflict."

Matilda always had a great love for children, but sadly she was never able to conceive. She still works part time in a day care. Children sometimes can make an abusive marriage more bearable, but Matilda had no one but herself at home with her husband.

When she felt rageful toward Leon, Matilda said, "I always considered the consequences. I didn't want to be sitting in jail." Matilda figures she used alcohol to suppress the pain of the abuse, to not feel. "I was able to put up with the abuse. When I drank I couldn't get angry."

Matilda, a religious woman, had stopped drinking about fifteen years before her cancer, so she experienced several years of abuse without the softening of alcohol. Substance abusers use alcohol or drugs to not feel, to detach from life.

Matilda described an incident that "put the icing on the cake." She had used Leon's car to go to her job caring for disabled clients. He was possessive of his vehicles, particularly of the one she used, but she had no other way of getting to her work that day. When he came home from work (fully sober), the tirade of abuse began in the front yard. He finally went into the house and Matilda apparently blacked out from rage. "The next thing I know he was on the floor in the other room and I was on top of him choking him. The cast iron skillet was on the floor next to us. I don't remember hitting him. All I know is that he got up a changed man." Leon hadn't gotten the expected reaction from Matilda and apparently had a new respect for her strength. The term "frying pan" (perhaps inappropriately) became the source of hilarity in our women's group. When a member described incidents of abusive behavior, someone inevitably would chime in "time for the frying pan." This was our own special cue that something needed to change.

Matilda's husband continued to drink episodically and be verbally abusive, but he never laid a hand on her again. When he retired after many years in a stressful and physically demanding job about five years ago, he became "another person" capable of expressing appreciation to Matilda.

Some years after joining the group, Matilda confided what had helped her stop drinking long ago. She credits God with giving her strength to change Leon's behavior and "give up the drink."

Matilda does not take credit for Leon's transformation. "I pulled through this with the hands of God. He was by my side." She recalls the last time she drank alcohol. During the time she was trying to quit, she bought two nips while driving. She drank the first and stopped for a red light and was about to drink the second one. "All of a sudden, I was enveloped in darkness and knew God was present and I needed to change. When I could see once more, I never again had the wish to drink…God took the taste for alcohol away. God brought me through this. I was anointed by God to get through this and He is always by my side."

Chapter 5
Caregivers: The Club Sandwich Generation
Patricia

A TALL, ARTSY looking woman with flowing hair and funky clothes and jewelry entered my therapy office over twelve years ago with complaints of "toxic worry" about what she called her Three Fates.

I looked at her curiously and asked for an explanation. In therapy we're privileged to often meet fascinating, intelligent people. Toni happened to be one of these clients. In every session with Toni I'm educated with a new term related to literature, Greek mythology, or art. That isn't surprising, because Toni is a seventy-three year old graduate of a prestigious women's college with a master's degree from an Ivy League University. She teaches at a small liberal arts college where she is a tenured English department faculty member.

In our first session Toni spoke of the Three Fates as Greek mythological figures. The Fates were three female deities who shaped people's lives. In particular, they influenced human destiny and determined how long a person would live. They were referred to in Greek mythology as The Spinner, The Allotter, and The Unavoidable. The fates were said to control the thread of each person's life: They spun the thread, measured it out, and cut it with a pair of shears to end the life span.

When I asked Toni how this related to her life she said, "I live with and care for my aging mother, I am constantly annoyed by my younger sister, and I worry about my daughter." She complained that the three of them would be the death of her.

I told myself, "That sounds depressing." Those are the subliminal messages that float above my head in little bubbles when I meet a new client. It wasn't time to say these things out loud. Instead, I asked Toni how long she'd felt this chronic worry.

"My entire life," she answered. She went on to say that as a young girl she needed to care for her mother, thanks to her mother's depression and her father's good-natured helplessness.

Her sister, four years younger, was a troubled young woman with mental health issues that started in college and continued to the present. While growing up Toni often had to manage the household and care for her sister. She lived in constant insecurity and fear that something negative would happen to a family member and the family would be destitute.

During my therapy with Toni I realized she had always been in a caretaker role, from caring for her mother, to her sister, then to a husband. She did enjoy her college years at an all women's prestigious New England school, although her fun-loving time was short lived when her sister enrolled in the same college when Toni was a junior. Then she needed to care for her sister, who had a nervous breakdown during her freshman year.

Toni married the summer after graduating college and immediately became a housewife to a young, up and coming professional she was introduced to on a blind date. She married Jack because, as she put it, "That's what you were supposed to do in 1962 after you finished college." Soon she was a mother with two children and they lived in a small town in New Hampshire. She told me without much emotion that the first ten years of marriage went well; she and Jack were a contented couple raising their son and daughter. She settled into the life as the wife of a successful professional and enjoyed her years raising the children. However, she related with some sadness that in the second decade their marriage began to show signs of wear and tear; Jack stayed later at the office and pulled away from family time. Toni feared he was having an affair, but had no proof until her husband came to her after twenty-two years of marriage and announced, "I'm leaving you. I've been involved with my secretary for many years and she is carrying my child."

Poof! Jack was gone. Her son had left for college and her daughter was a junior in high school. Toni felt terrified and her chronic worrying returned. How would she survive? Where would she live? She couldn't afford to keep their big house. Jack quickly moved out and lived with his girlfriend. The divorce occurred quickly so he could marry his "new love." Toni knew his secretary was no new love, but what could she do? The marriage was over.

Toni dug deep, reminding herself she was intelligent and well educated, even though she'd never had a profession. Her college degree in art history wouldn't get her far, so what could she do? Struggling with anxiety, she turned to the strength of her academic prowess and enrolled at a local Ivy League college where she earned a master's degree in literature with a high honors ranking. Her daughter was off in college by then and for the first time in Toni's life she lived on her own. She loved it and felt successful. She began teaching at a local community college and got rave reviews from her students. She was happy, and although she sometimes worried about money, she was free of toxic worry.

But these worry-free years were short lived, because when she was fifty-three her father died and her mother needed Toni to come live with her. Without a husband, her mom couldn't manage emotionally and financially to cope with life. Toni immediately took on the responsibility. Toni's sister lived in New York City and was not willing to move. Toni returned to her family home and secured a job teaching at a small liberal arts college.

By the time Toni started therapy with me she felt exhausted by a lifetime of emotional and financial responsibilities. At that time Toni was sixty-one, her mother was ninety-two, her sister was fifty-seven, and her daughter was thirty-two years of age with a twenty month old son. I felt a deep sense of concern and compassion for Toni. She was the "good doobie" who took on the responsibility of making everyone else happy, yet so readily gave up feeling she deserved to be happy herself.

Toni began by talking about her daughter Jennifer, who was her greatest concern. Jennifer had married a hotel administrator a few years earlier—a man Toni could barely tolerate. She called him lazy and weird. I felt uncomfortable with how she degraded her son-in-law and thought she might be sabotaging her daughter's marriage by her constant criticism. Toni reassured me she kept her comments about him to herself. I wondered if that was possible.

Toni's son was also married. He had a professional degree like his father and was self-sufficient and independent, as was his college educated wife.

Toni didn't worry about her son or daughter-in-law. But she carried a massive amount of anxiety about her daughter and son-in-law. My first therapeutic approach was to try and help create a realistic picture of how overly invested Toni was in her daughter's life. She agreed to a certain extent, but explained that her daughter had always been impulsive and made bad choices. She also had sympathy for her daughter, because she felt the daughter had never been valued by her father. Toni tried to make up for this lack of fatherly love with her smothering tendencies. When her grandson was born Toni believed it was her responsibility to make sure he was healthy and happy. I was concerned about her over investment in her grandson's well-being and encouraged her to give her daughter space and allow her to become a competent mother on her own. I began to realize that Toni invested so much time in her daughter's life because she (Toni) had not been investing in her own life.

I told myself, "This is going to be a lesson in dis-engagement from her daughter, as well as active life composition for Toni."

At first glance, Toni appeared to be an overly stressed woman in the classic role of caretaker with a sandwich generation scenario. But, Toni's life was more than the typical three generation sandwich of caring for an aging parent and her own children. She created a club sandwich by adding the layer of a grandson.

As I listened to Toni's story that first day, I realized she had a codependent relationship with each generation of women in her life: her mother, her sister, and her daughter. As a psychologist I knew this would be a tangled web to unweave. I knew I needed patience and understanding to help Toni with the complicated task of lovingly disengaging from these family members and seeking more personal happiness.

Self-help author Melody Beattie defines codependency as the need to be in control of other peoples' lives at the expense of taking care of yourself. I often use her book, *Codependent No More*,[4] as a resource in my clinical practice. I recommended this book to Toni as part of her therapy because it offers straightforward insights into the complex world of codependency.

We most often use the term codependency to describe the loved ones of alcoholics or drug users—people who accept the troubles and worries of others as their own instead of developing the ability to separate from issues and emotions without discarding the relationship with the person.

For example, suppose your husband wakes up with a terrific hangover from binging the night before. He obviously can't function at work, so you call his boss and tell a lie instead of making your husband face the consequences. You tell yourself, "We can't survive if he loses his job, so I have to help him." Doing this can make us feel noble in the short term, but it isn't a healthy way to live.

Codependency doesn't always involve addiction. In many ways we're all codependent to some extent in one relationship or another. But the problem arises when putting too much of ourselves into relationships begins to make us unhappy, unfulfilled, and even physically ill. A fine line exists between caring for our loved ones, versus worrying ourselves sick about them and trying to control and direct their behavior.

After hearing Toni's story my first step was trying to help her deal with the intense, health threatening anxiety created by her relationships. I suggested yoga and deep breathing exercises, and provided reading materials on codependency. We worked on healthy living habits, such as a good night's sleep, nutritious eating, and daily exercise. At first, Toni dismissed these ideas as just common sense and didn't think they pertained to her. With an iron grip she held on, maintaining control of her anxiety by controlling other people's lives. Again I tried to be patient with Toni, but as she continued coming to my office with irritable bowel syndrome, headaches, aching knees, and an aching back, I persevered in counseling healthy living habits.

---

4   Beattie, Melody, *Codependent No More: How to Stop Controlling Others and Start Caring for Yourself*, New York: Harper Collins, Hazeldon Foundation, 1987.

Over the next few months I noticed Toni entering my office with a jauntier gait and smiling a bit more. When I asked if she was doing anything different, she said, "Well, I did join a gym and I'm enjoying the classes." When I asked which classes, Toni said, "I took your advice on yoga and I love it. I actually get to quiet my mind for a few minutes and my body feels more limber and relaxed."

I was so thrilled I felt like jumping for joy. Hurrah! Toni was taking care of herself. I also noticed Toni was talking less about her daughter's life during our therapy sessions and more about her coursework and how she enjoyed her fellow teachers.

In time Toni's panic over her daughter's life began to subside, but issues with her mother intensified. Now approaching 98 years, Miriam, had physical and mental problems. The challenge of caring for her was a major worry for Toni—especially leaving Miriam alone in the house. Toni's mother was no longer able to navigate the stairs in their Victorian home. Toni was terrified her mother would fall and break a hip, or worse. Miriam would forget to turn off the stove and sometimes wandered out of the house thinking she needed to get groceries. She tried having someone stay with Miriam when she was at work, but Miriam was rude and rebellious with the caretakers. No one wanted to take this kind of abuse.

I tried to help Toni with senior care services I knew about in our community, but that was a dead end. Soon, Miriam had trouble managing her toileting, bathing, and other self-care needs. Toni had to think about an assisted living nursing care center for her mother. Moving Miriam to a care facility was a huge step for Toni, who still wanted to be her mother's caretaker. I was worried this could be a difficult transition for Toni and her mother. And then one day Toni came to therapy and, with great surprise in her voice, told me her mother had suggested it was time for her to live in a nursing care facility. Miriam, who was never much on compliments, said to Toni one night over dinner, "Toni, you've been a wonderful daughter, but at age ninety-nine it's time for me to leave this old house. I can't make the stairs and I know it's a worry for you. I'm ready to make the move."

Wow! This came as a surprise for both Toni and me, but we were both relieved. With my encouragement, Toni found an excellent assisted living facility where her mother made a fine adjustment. Fortunately, Miriam made the change without adding more guilt to Toni's life.

Toni visited her mother daily after work and continued to be her caretaker in a loving, supportive way, rather than taking on the responsibility of full care. Toni always brought a special snack, a book for her mom to read, or a small surprise. She still cared, but without the anxiety of meeting all her mother's needs. Her mother died peacefully two years later at one hundred and one years of age. Toni had released the first of her Three Fates. Yet she continued to worry.

Toni's relationship with her sister and daughter, her other "two fates," continued to challenge her in different ways. From our discussions I knew Toni as a wise saver and investor. She used extra teaching jobs and paintings she sold to keep herself afloat in the old family homestead—and to help her daughter. In time Toni decided to sell the house, partly to unload the burden of home ownership and repairs, and also to give her younger sister Ellie half of the proceeds.

Ellie had always worried Toni. Their relationship was still fraught with arguments and upheavals because Ellie was contrary most of the time. She would not financially contribute to upkeep of the family homestead and wouldn't clean out her belongings so the house could be sold. While their mother was alive Ellie didn't help with her care, yet she liked to criticize Toni for not doing the right things for Miriam. An actress, who taught theater courses, Ellie lived in a rent controlled New York City apartment. To Toni's dismay, shortly after Miriam died, her emotionally fragile sister began to show signs of dementia.

Toni felt panic at the thought of her sister moving back into the family home. This idea created frequent bouts of anticipatory anxiety—worrying about what might happen and creating scenarios in her mind. I suggested she talk to Ellie and see if this was in her sister's plans. Sometimes Toni got caught up with obsessive worrying in her head and brought herself to the point of panic before exploring the issue. When she spoke with Ellie, she was relieved to hear that Ellie planned to stay in NYC for the rest of her life.

Toni then tried coaxing Ellie to look into subsidized housing for actors and actresses, but her sister would have none of this. Toni worried and worried about her sister's fate, given her failing memory and cognitive abilities. She scheduled a neuro-psychological evaluation for Ellie to check for signs of early onset dementia. But before that date arrived Toni received a call from a NYC hospital that her sister had a massive stroke and was on life support.

Toni went through agonizing days while she wrestled with taking her brain dead sister off life support. She felt guilt over years of viewing her sister as a burden, and she felt deep sorrow to see her sister beyond hope.

Only after Ellie died did Toni realize her sister had a wonderful support network from her synagogue and in her work and acting community. Her sister actually led a full, independent life with many friends and rich cultural experiences. Toni also learned Ellie had done a fairly good job of squirreling away money, and Toni was the sole heir.

What a turn of event—from utter dread about her sister's future to feeling financially at ease, thanks to Ellie's final gift. The Second Fate was put to rest. I hoped Toni would see how she had been worrying FOR NOTHING. I wanted to jump up and down on my office sofa, like Tom Cruise did on the Oprah Winfrey show, and scream, "See you had nothing to worry about, Toni! Stop worrying so much."

I didn't perform acrobatics in my office, but I did start discussing with Toni how much she had needlessly worried. She began to gain insight into her need to worry.

She said, "If I don't worry, I'm afraid something awful will happen."

I asked, "Like what?"

She paused, "Well, like someone will die, or I won't have enough money to survive, or . . . I will lose control."

Aha! Toni finally heard herself say her fears out loud, and she started to laugh. "Everyone is going to die someday, and I have plenty of money. So shoot, maybe I should try to stop this needless worry."

I nodded and said, "Let's keep talking about this in the next session."

Now Toni faced the Third Fate—her daughter Jennifer, who had finally divorced after five years of unhappy marriage. Toni felt relieved to some extent, but now worried about her daughter's finances. Toni had helped Jennifer with rent, even when she herself was on a tight budget. She told me this was more about keeping a roof over her grandson's head than caring for her daughter. I wasn't sure this was totally the case, but I didn't confront Toni because I felt she needed to do what she needed to do. I just said, "At some point Jennifer is going to have to live without you."

She looked at me sadly and said, "I know. I've been thinking about that more and more since Ellie died."

My job was to be supportive and give advice as necessary, not to judge Toni's life choices. Jennifer earned a meager living teaching exercise and dance, and Toni felt it was her duty to assist as needed. As long as her daughter was trying and working, Toni was going to help her and her grandson. In fact, Toni invested thousands of dollars into a dance/exercise studio that barely stayed afloat.

Obviously I had an opinion about all this, but it wasn't my place as a psychologist to press the point with Toni. When a client is managing financially and making reasonably sound judgments, it isn't my job to decide how she should spend money. I knew Toni still had a codependent relationship with her daughter, but it wasn't for me to argue this point. In fact, she heard that opinion from plenty of other people in her life. Instead, therapy at this point focused on making sure Toni was still doing active, positive, and healthy things for herself. She assured me she was still exercising and spending time with friends. She went on a trip to Spain with a college room-mate and had started painting again.

I was thrilled to tell her, "Great, Toni! I'm so glad you're spending money on yourself and giving yourself fun."

She laughed at me and said, "Dr. Martin, you will never tell me not to do something for myself, will you?"

I reflected and said, "Toni, I think it's about time you start enjoying your life and having fun!"

She chuckled and said, "I'll try."

After her sister's death, Toni decided to buy a home for her daughter and grandson. She would make a room for herself in the house to use on her monthly visits. Toni also saw this as a possible future living space for part of the year after she retired. In any case, she thought it sounded like a good real estate investment, and would give her daughter and grandson a safe, permanent residence. Presently, this arrangement is working, so Toni has (for the time being) tied up loose ends with her Third Fate.

Over the years of therapy Toni taught me the difference between codependency and family love. I realize that many times she crossed the line and took responsibility for others' behavior. Yet I also began understanding that when you love another person, at times you need to step in and lend a helping hand—even if it seems to be a codependent hand.

At last I see that Toni's behavior is healthier because she adjusted her life to help her daughter and grandson without harming herself or taking on excessive burdens. Toni is beginning to talk about retirement and where she wants to live. Just discussing it seems to lift her spirits. She is exploring an artists' colony in Florida where she can paint and write.

I look at her with a twinkle in my eye, and say, "That sounds great, Toni!"

She grins at me. "You know, Doc, it's about time I have some fun, isn't it?"

Was that a little skip in her step as Toni left my office? Yep, I think so! Toni has lived a full life, enriched with teaching and travel, caring for her mother and daughter, and loving a difficult sister. She wasn't afraid to let herself give and care for others when she heard the fates calling.

Codependent? At times, perhaps. But . . . who knows what lies ahead!

Resources:

Codependency is defined as "a psychological condition or a relationship in which a person is controlled or manipulated by another who is affected with a pathological condition (typically narcissism or drug addiction); and in broader terms, it refers to the dependence on the needs of, or control by, another." Wikipedia

www.mentalhealthamerica.net
www.psychcentral.com
www.apa.com

Chapter 6
I Found My Sisters: Women's Friendships
Helene

I'VE ALWAYS ENVIED friends who are close with their sisters: talking on the phone, shopping together, traveling together, and reminiscing about childhood adventures. I don't dwell on my sadness, but when I see happy sisters together I sometimes miss being close to my own sister.

She and I are almost six years apart in age. She was born first, early in our parents' marriage during an unhappy time. When my sister was eighteen months old our mother was hospitalized for a year with tuberculosis. At a crucial time in her childhood, my sister was separated from our mother—and also from our father, who was trying to run a business. Separation like that is bound to interrupt the parent-child bonding and contribute to insecurity in the child.

I was born during a more joyful time in my parents' lives and always felt loved and cherished. During my sister's early years the family moved often, which disrupted her schooling and friendships. I was fortunate to live in the same town from fourth grade to graduation. My sense of security allowed me to become more outgoing than my sister. I believed I could accomplish anything if I worked hard enough. I focused my energy on educational goals outside the family and continued to feel supported and appreciated by my parents. Sadly, I didn't put nearly as much energy into the relationship with my sister, who was married and had a child while I was still in college.

After talking with hundreds of women over the years I know it isn't unusual to lack closeness with sisters and brothers. Just as we don't always click with people at work or school, sometimes our personalities don't mesh within the family. This is no one's fault; it just is. Some of my patients tell me they feel they don't belong in their families—and the old saying of the stork dropping the baby in the wrong nest comes to mind.

I've come to accept and understand my relationship with my sister, whom I love despite the lack of closeness. I know she loves me, though we are not best friends. Fortunately, I've been blessed with many sister-like women in my life.

Sister can mean having the same parents, and that's how I saw it for many years. But as defined in the online *Free Dictionary,* a sister can be many other things, including "a close woman friend or companion." That's how I define *sister.* I have a sister-in-law sister in Brooklyn, a retired nurse sister in Half Moon Bay, a high school classmate sister in Georgia, a nursing school sister in LA and, of course, my writing partner sister, Patricia. My UCC church has provided sisters of all ages. I became close with one of my older "sisters" when we shared memorable weekend family retreats on the Cape. I quietly watched her parent a brood of highly individual, active, and charismatic children with a long leash, while modeling kindness, responsibility, and moral values. Our families have shared confirmations, graduations, weddings, births, illness, and deaths. We share personal issues with trust that they will go no further. I feel blessed to have this relationship.

Sadly, in our society, when the stress of life closes in and we face conflicting demands from family and career, friendships may be the first thing we neglect. However, these friendships with other women—our sisters—could be the very thing that saves us. Not only are friendships among women fulfilling, fun, supportive, and an opportunity for role modeling, but recent studies confirm that women with a strong social network live longer. When women feel stress, we are chemically engineered to tend to our children and gather around other women— called the tend-and-befriend response by researchers.[5] This social behavior is linked to decreased health problems and longer, more fulfilling lives.[6]

Yet, how quick we are to discard other women when a man is waiting in the wings. Think of all the sit-coms and movies that show women kicking their girlfriends to the curb when a new boyfriend is on the horizon; sad but true. No matter what's going on in my life, I try to maintain and expand my circle of deep friendships with other women; friendships that sustain and protect me during the storms of my life.

I hope you will visit the website and blog called "Women I Want to Grow Old With" (www.womeniwanttogrowoldwith.com) which addresses women's need to

---

5   Taylor, S.E.,Cousino Klein, L et al, "Behavioral responses to stress in females: tend-and-befriend, not fight-or-flight." *Psychological Review* 2000, Vol. 107, No.3, 411-429.

---

6   Achat, H., Kawachi,I et al, "Social networks, stress and health-related quality of life." *Quality of Life Research* 1998, Dec;7(8):735-50.

nurture friendships and recognizes the importance of these friendships to a happy, healthy, and productive life.

I wish for you the presence of many sisters in your life!

This poem by Barbara Ardinger expresses the value of sisterhood and is used with her permission.

There is a Web of Women

There is a web of women living lightly in the world.
As gently as hand upon forehead, checking for fever,
the web touches the pulse of the planet with intention
to help
to heal
to comfort.
There is a flood of women weeping softly for the world.
As tender as hand upon heart, cherishing her precious children,
the web cries for lost intention
to heal
to comfort
to help.
There is a circle of women dancing joyfully through the world.
As exultant as hand touching yoni, celebrating our mysteries,
the web sings for intention found again
to comfort
to help
to heal.
There is a web of women tenderly enclosing the world.
As sturdy as hands setting roots, planting community,
the web encircles intention held
to help
to heal
to comfort.

Chapter 7
The Power of the Therapy Group

Helene

I HAVE ALWAYS enjoyed leading therapy groups. Forming a new group is especially exciting, from deciding who should attend to "opening night" when members meet for the first time and share their stories. The sharing of the stories is what either ropes in the members or chases them away. When new members can find common ground and sense people are listening without judgment, chances are good they will return. The leaders walk a fine line by encouraging participation, yet being careful not to let one person dominate the time, or worse yet, "spill the beans" and reveal so much that in hindsight she feels humiliated and never returns.

Experts have explained why the power of the group has changed people who were otherwise stuck in individual therapy and dysfunctional relationship patterns. Sharing stories helps us feel less alone, less damaged. The group process offers hope. It is an opportunity for members and leaders to learn from one another and be exposed to healthier role models. The group gives us an opportunity to express worries and emotions that are often withheld from family and friends. Members can experience a sense of being nurtured and supported beyond what their families can provide. They learn how to communicate with people of different ages, backgrounds, and life experiences. I have often explained group therapy as a safe laboratory where we can practice behavior and take risks.

The success of every group depends on the expertise, confidence, and style of the leader. I've had co-leaders who adopted a Freud like analytic posture and clearly placed themselves in a superior position to the members. This traditional (dare I say old-fashioned) approach made me uncomfortable, so I can imagine how the patients felt. Long silences (loooooooong silences) occurred while group members stared at the floor. The only sound was the shifting of weight in the chairs.

My best group therapy experience came from working with a licensed social worker who specialized in substance abuse and recovery issues. We decided to develop a codependency group for women who were stuck in relationships and were enabling significant people in their lives to continue patterns of abuse. Sometimes the relationships were abusive and sometimes substance abuse was a factor. My co-leader's style of leading was far different from my earlier colleague. He was open, jolly, and did not put a wall between himself and the patients. He wasn't afraid to let us know he had personal experience with his own struggles.

The book *Codependent No More* by Melody Beattie is important reading for those of us who are trying to change our behavior and escape codependent traps. She gives concrete guidance and helped develop the codependency arm of the 12 step recovery programs.

At the time we developed the group in our out-patient setting, we had many women in our caseloads who were codependent. One woman divorced the emotionally abusive father of her children and found herself profoundly depressed and obsessed with him. Another woman was married to a serial philanderer who learned the art of cheating while stationed away from his family in far off places. She developed a severe panic disorder while trying to single parent two challenging sons and suppress her suspicions about her husband. Her unhealthy codependent behaviors exploded when she became her own private detective, as many do. She located his truck at a local motel, burst into the room, found him with a woman in bed, and threatened him with his own gun. Several other group members struggled with children who were substance abusers. Hearing the members' dramatic stories always caught the group's attention and brought words of support. Other members would acknowledge they had the same patterns of behavior. Some of the patients who were most stuck and entrenched in their own codependent patterns offered the most insight into other's behavior.

I still have one of those original group members with me today—now in a tiny group of three mothers of addicts. A number of years ago and several years after the codependency group adjourned, I began saying to these three women whom I saw individually, that I heard their stories almost word for word from other women. I already felt as though they were gathering in my office, so they agreed to meet as a group. A fourth woman who would have benefitted could never bring herself to come. She was of Irish-American origin and still influenced by the "don't hang your dirty laundry in public" philosophy. Sadly, that viewpoint keeps many people from the benefits of therapy groups, 12 step programs, individual therapy, and even close friendships.

Two of the women who do attend the group are also Irish-American and it has taken them years to fully open up and address painful issues. We are a tight little band of four who have survived deaths, imprisoned children, aging parents, abusive marriages, children's addictions, and some joys as well; in marriages and grandchildren. We are teary one week, laughing the next, but always respectful of each other's struggles and offering empathy. I hope these women will stay in touch after our meetings come to an end and continue to support each other.

The famous psychiatrist and author Irvin D. Yalom wrote a seminal text: *The Theory and Practice of Group Psychotherapy.*[7] While explaining why groups are so powerful and curative, Dr. Yalom spoke of altruism (the unselfish caring for others). In his discussion of altruism, he opens with this allegory that expresses what happens in group therapy:

"There is an old Hasidic story of the Rabbi who had a conversation with the Lord about Heaven and Hell. 'I will show you Hell,' said the Lord and led the Rabbi into a room in the middle of which was a very big, round table. The people sitting at it were famished and desperate. In the middle of the table was a large pot of stew, enough and more for everyone. The smell of the stew was delicious and made the Rabbi's mouth water. The people round the table were holding spoons with long handles. Each one found it was just possible to reach the pot to take a spoonful of stew, but because the handle of his spoon was longer than a man's arm, he could not get the food back in his mouth. The Rabbi saw that their suffering was terrible. 'Now I will show you heaven,' said the Lord, and they went into another room, exactly the same as the first. There was the same big, round table and the same pot of stew. The people as before, were equipped with the same long-handled spoons—but here they were well-nourished and plump, laughing and talking. At first the Rabbi did not understand. 'It is simple, but it requires a certain skill,' said the Lord. 'You see they learn to feed each other.'"

---

7   Yalom, Irvin D., MD, *The Theory and Practice of Group Psychotherapy*, (New York: Basic Books, 1975), 3-17.

Chapter 8
To Forgive, But Not Forget

Patricia

AT SOME TIME in our lives, each of us has been hurt, offended or treated badly by someone. How do we manage anger and resentment? The movie, *Philomena*, based on the true life story of Philomena Lee, tackles the difficult issue of wrongdoing and its consequences on a human life. If you haven't seen the movie, I won't spoil your viewing by going over the details of what Philomena faced as she searched for the son she gave up for adoption during the 1950s. Suffice to say, the film is a morality tale about evil and forgiveness.

As a clinical psychologist in private practice for 30 years, I've counseled thousands of men, women, and children about life concerns. One of the foremost issues for many people is lugging around the pain from past injuries or carrying guilt for past transgressions. Learning to forgive others as well as ourselves is a monumental task, yet necessary if we want to find peace in our lives.

What should we do with the feelings of anger and resentment we harbor toward those who hurt us? What if the guilty person is dead and never apologized? What if you know the offender will never say, "I'm sorry?" What if you get a blanket apology, but you don't feel it's sincere or specific enough to truly acknowledge the injury? What if the person who offended you doesn't recognize he (or she) did anything wrong—and you know that person will never understand your feelings?

If you carry the pain and hurt from such injuries and it's making you angry, depressed, or physically ill, I suggest you forgive. This forgiveness is for yourself, not for the other person. I like to see the word as two words: For Give. Take the hurt and anger, put it in your hands, and give it away. If you want to hurl it; hurl it. If you want to blow it out of your hand like a feather; do so. If you want to slam it to the ground and stomp on it; do so. But what you need to do is take the pain outside of you and give it back. Return it to the offender. Hand it back to the universe. Don't keep it inside hurting you. By giving it over, you set yourself free. Saying "I forgive you," to yourself or another may take years; it may take work in therapy; it may take a lifetime. But I believe this is a necessary step toward finding inner peace.

For some, forgiveness may be difficult and almost impossible. When you live in fear of a person who has physically, mentally, or emotionally abused you, forgiveness is elusive. When you fear someone who still has the power to hurt you, forgiving is difficult. You won't feel safe enough to forgive until the other person is totally removed from your life. If you are in the circumstances of continued fear, don't feel wrong or ashamed if you aren't ready, or able, to forgive.

To forgive does not mean condoning someone's bad actions. This is a common error in people's thinking and is why many of us can't forgive. We say, "I'll never believe what that person did to me was right." By forgiving, you do not overlook, accept, or excuse the pain someone inflicted upon you. But you do remove it as a burden you carry. You can "For Give." You can let go of the pain you feel inside by releasing it from your load.

If a transgression is criminal, then you can seek justice through our legal system. This may help you feel you've done something constructive to eradicate evil in this world. But, the justice system does not produce forgiveness. That is only accomplished on an individual, personal level.

What about "forgive and forget?" The word forgive is frequently paired with forget, but forgetting isn't always necessary or desirable—especially when the transgressor has not made a sincere apology and acknowledged the wrongdoing. If you forget before true contrition is displayed you may set yourself up to be harmed again. When evil has been done, it's necessary to remember and record in order to make sure the harmful behavior doesn't happen again. If someone injured you, you can forgive, but remember this person has the potential to harm you again. Unless you received a genuine apology—an acknowledgement of wrongdoing—and the person is taking steps to change, you may need to dissolve the relationship or remove yourself from further contact with that person. If we don't acknowledge the evil, we are not taking the necessary steps to ward off wrongdoing in the future.

If you have the opportunity to see the movie you will witness active forgiveness and also observe one woman's conscious choice to record and remember evil so it won't happen again.

As Philomena said, "I forgive you because I don't want to remain angry."[8]

---

8   This chapter is taken in part from the article, *"Philomena" Sends Right Message About Forgiveness,* published in Mass-Live, March 10, 2014.

Stories of Survival

Chapter 9
Survivor Guilt
Patricia

JANET, A DIMINUTIVE blond with a short-cropped hair style, entered my office complaining about a miserable marriage to a man she could barely tolerate at this point. When I met Janet, she and her husband were fifteen years into their marriage and had a thirteen year old son named Will.

Janet told me she had an affair a few years earlier in an attempt to find friendship, emotional support, attention, and caring. Her husband Bob found out about it, but instead of divorcing her he chose to stay with the marriage and torture her about the infidelity. Janet ended the affair in hopes of improving her marriage. Instead, Bob refused counseling, and would ignore Janet most of the time, walking by her within their home without speaking. When he did speak to Janet it was in monosyllabic sentences, like "yep, nope, maybe." He was clearly punishing her, in a passive aggressive manner. He wasn't interested in sex and when Janet tried to make any gesture of physical warmth, Bob would snidely say, "Go get that from your boyfriend." As the saying goes, "he buried the hatchet, but kept the handle within easy reach."

At this point Janet didn't want a divorce because she thought the breakup would be hard on her son and she feared a divorce was something she would later regret.

When I expressed my surprise that she stayed in such a miserable situation, Janet told me she had trouble with the finality of ending relationships and doubted her own ability to make decisions. Janet told me of several friendships with women that sounded down-right abusive. These were women she met at a "newcomers club" when she first moved to town when her son was an infant. Clearly these women only wanted her friendship so they could use her swimming pool or get free lunches. These so-called friends would constantly drop by unannounced in the summer months to "take a dip" in Janet's pool, and then would stay all day—or worse yet, would ask Janet to watch their kids while they ran errands. When they returned two hours later with freshly painted toe nails and manicures it was clear Janet was being used as a free babysitter while they pampered themselves.

When I asked why she put up with this, Janet again said she just couldn't say no to people. I wondered why she allowed her husband and "friends" to use her this way. When Janet told me her life story, I began to realize her unhappy marriage and bogus friendships were actually symptoms of something much deeper—something that caused her to have difficulty with endings.

She was troubled by survivor's guilt.

Janet was the middle child of three, raised by a beloved father who was a minister and active in the civil rights movement. Janet had great love and admiration for her father, but her mother was another story. Janet described her as selfish, whiney, and self-indulgent. Her parent's marriage ended with the death of her father when Janet was sixteen. Unbeknownst to Janet, this event helped keep her stuck in her own unhappy marriage.

The father died when their family was on a religious retreat at a lakeside camp in upstate New York, during the summer of Janet's sixteenth birthday. She was having a wonderful time, loving the adventure of camping and making new friends. Her father, who was a swimmer in college, had invited another minister on a boat ride with him and Janet on a lovely summer day. They stopped the boat to go swimming in the lake, but Janet stayed on board because she had her period and was using pads rather than tampons. Suddenly, the boat started rocking and a freak squall came through. Janet had no idea how to run the boat, but her father shouted from the water for her to lower the step ladder over the side. She did that and watched her father push the overweight minister into the boat. Janet, a tiny, five foot teenager, pulled the man in with all her strength. When he awkwardly flipped into the boat, she reached down to get her father, but he was nowhere in sight. Janet searched frantically from every side of the boat; but, she couldn't find him. After that final memory, her mind goes blank.

Janet had no idea how she and the other minister returned back to the camping site. She was clearly in shock. The lake patrol didn't find her father's body until two days later on a distant shore of the lake.

Years later, Janet sobbed as she told the story in my office. After the accident, no one asked her what happened or encouraged her to tell the story. All the grieving and comforting focused on her mother, a new widow with three children. Janet was left to carry her own grief, along with guilt about her father's death. After that she became promiscuous throughout high school and college. As with many young women, promiscuity was actually a "cry out" for attention and love. Janet no longer received attention at home because her father was dead and her mother was busy with a new husband and their Brady Bunch combined family of six children. Janet had to fend for herself.

She found quick fixes of "love" in one night stands, with no fear of being rejected because she left without a commitment. As graduation from college approached she decided to marry Bob because she felt he was the best of the losers she dated. She didn't want to return to her mother's house and marrying Bob seemed her best option at the time. She knew the day she married him it was a mistake, but she went through with it anyway, still not realizing she needed to grieve for her father.

Once Janet spoke about the boating accident, she began the grieving process. During a year of therapy we sorted through her complicated feelings of sadness and guilt. With tenacity and courage, Janet pulled through. She then went on to divorce her husband and began rebuilding a relationship with her mother and brothers. She has since remarried to a kind, loving man (much like her father) and is happier than she has ever been.

Only one last bit of business is incomplete: The other survivor of the boating accident, the minister Janet pulled aboard, has contacted her after forty years and wants to meet with her. That work still lies ahead for Janet.

Survivor Guilt is defined as an intense feeling of guilt that occurs when a person believes she has done wrong by surviving a situation where others died. In many cases, we take responsibility for things over which we actually had no control. This is especially true for children, who may not understand all the circumstances surrounding an incident, but hold themselves responsible. Survivor guilt often leads to self-punishment, crippling depression, and self-blame.

Survivor guilt is actually empathy or selflessness twisted back upon oneself. People who feel this way often have the best human qualities—kindness, love, concern, and care. But psychological trauma can turn these wonderful qualities into dark, self-punishing attributes.

As with Janet, the guilt feelings may be hidden, but still affect our quality of life by attracting the wrong kind of relationships and keeping us stuck in depression and negative behaviors.

Resources:
www.bandbacktogether.com

Movie about survivor guilt: "Ordinary People" with Mary Tyler Moore, Timothy Hutton and Donald Sutherland (1980), and directed by Robert Redford. This movie is adapted from the novel by Judith Guest. It tells the story of a family ravaged by the tragic death of one son, with the surviving son suffering from the syndrome of survivor guilt. The masterful therapeutic work of a therapist, played by Judd Hirsch, demonstrates the healing work of therapy for someone troubled by survivor guilt.

Chapter 10
Surviving Panic Disorder: How Xanax Saved a Life
Helene

THE WORD THAT best describes Tammy when I first met her is *spunky*. She has always been a straight shooting woman with raspy, clipped speech, sparkling blue eyes and a blond pixie haircut. Her diminutive size contrasts with her huge heart and spirit. Tammy describes herself as "a hard nut to crack." This is the story of my twenty year relationship with Tammy.

I met Tammy ten years after she was diagnosed with panic disorder with agoraphobia just before she left her twenty year marriage. Her anxiety disorder developed in reaction to growing up with an alcoholic father and then marrying Stan, an emotionally abusive husband. She worked with him in the family restaurant business while raising their two sons, Michael and Steven.

"I couldn't do anything right," she said, to explain the marital conflicts. Her husband would humiliate her at the restaurant with disparaging remarks and demeaning demands. She never knew when something she did would precipitate a torrent of verbal abuse.

One thing she and Stan enjoyed doing together was watching their son Michael excel in ice hockey. Traveling to his away games and bonding with other parents brought rare happiness to the marriage. Sadly, Michael began abusing alcohol at age seventeen and quickly exploded into full blown alcoholism. Tammy recently admitted to me that she herself overused alcohol to deal with anxiety while in her twenties. She had a high tolerance for alcohol that amazed her friends at parties. Interestingly, people with anxiety disorders frequently use alcohol to manage their anxiety in social situations.

Tammy's tremendous panic attacks began at age twenty-seven. She and none of her medical providers could understand what caused her heart to race, her shortness of breath, and her terror at the thought of leaving the house. She was unable to go anywhere without someone with her. The dread of a panic attack became worse than the attack itself. She finally sought help at the out-patient psychiatric department of a large medical center. There she was diagnosed and treated by a psychiatrist who was familiar with panic disorder. He had begun using the then new drug Xanax which helped decrease anxiety. Because Xanax is a benzodiazepine and is contraindicated with alcohol, Tammy promised to stop drinking—and kept her word. The Xanax decreased her apprehension of panic attacks and became one of the tools that enabled her to develop an independent life.

When I took over Tammy's care I was aware of the growing disapproval for prescribing benzodiazepines by themselves. But we quickly learned she was unable to tolerate any medication besides Xanax for her anxiety disorder. When Prozac, and later other SSRI's came on the market in the late 1980s, many sufferers had significant decreases in their anxiety symptoms and panic attacks when these medications were prescribed. We prefer to use them or any other non-addictive antianxiety medicine rather than the benzodiazepines because of the potential for overuse, addiction, and diversion. There has always been a high street value on benzodiazepines.

When "benzos" first came on the scene, they were seen as a great panacea for the stress of that era. (Remember the song "Mother's Little Helper?" by the Rolling Stones?) In recent years many prescribers refuse to prescribe any medication classified as a benzodiazepine. No matter what other prescriptions we tried, Tammy developed an adverse reaction and her anxiety was intensified. The Xanax enabled her to be less intimidated by Stan while he was still with her, and when he finally left she was able to cope. He made the divorce process difficult and was unwilling to pay adequate support, despite her disability. Ultimately she became a housekeeper in a local hotel, utilizing her skills as a meticulous homemaker,

A year after the separation from her husband, Tammy learned he was gay. She found herself angry at him for hiding the true reason behind his contempt of her.

Her son Michael's alcoholism worsened as the years passed. He had countless detox admissions and bounced from one rehab center to another, never successfully maintaining sobriety. Tammy struggled as a parent, at times acknowledging she was an enabler by driving him places, going to court, and giving him money. I cautioned her about this behavior and encouraged her to go to AL-Anon to get support and advice from other family members of alcoholics.

Tammy was burdened with even more guilt and sadness when Michael revealed that his dad might have sexually abused him. Sadly, Michael died alone in his apartment twenty years after starting to drink. Tammy never gave up on him and would call regularly and help with groceries and necessities. Her last conversation with him was a loving one, which gave her some comfort. Although it broke her heart that he died alone, she was never weighed down by the guilt of having abandoned him.

While coping with Michael, Tammy's conscientiousness and hard work paid off with a promotion to head housekeeper. Unfortunately, her job was physically demanding and gave her chronic back pain.

One and one half years ago, two years after Michael's death, Tammy was diagnosed with stage III ovarian cancer. She dealt with the diagnosis bravely, just as she dealt with every tragic setback of her life. She was compliant with treatment and displayed dry wit throughout. Her cancer is currently in remission. Her pixie cut has returned, more gray than blond, but she is spunkier than ever. She reports that she is well liked by her health care providers. This is no surprise, because not only is she entertaining, she is also a compliant and conscientious patient. She knows her cancer is being treated as a chronic disease that may periodically return.

Tammy is working hard to strengthen her relationship with Steven, her second son. Both of them were devastated by Michael's death and both developed protective shields to ward off hurt. Steven's resentments for Michael ran deep. Steven was never an athlete like his brother, who won enthusiastic parental approval for his sports achievements, nor did Steven require the attention and support Michael received later on for his disability. Steven quietly supported his mother by financing the duplex they shared. The Biblical story of the prodigal son comes to mind in which the obedient, hardworking son is left in the dust when his irresponsible brother returns home. Steven responded with rage when Michael relapsed, and even when he died. One only can guess he was responding to the loss of a sibling relationship with his brother and the waste of enormous potential. Tammy and Steven had great difficulty speaking of Michael without becoming angry. Her sadness and regret clashed with Steven's unresolved rage.

Little by little, Tammy and Steven are beginning to comfort each other. Steven's fiancée has been instrumental in fostering their relationship. She tries to help them understand each other and helps both by attending important doctor's appointments with Tammy. She asks the important questions and takes notes.

Growing up in an alcoholic family set the stage for Tammy's panic disorder and led her to develop a protective shield. In such families the children never know what to expect and constantly live on the defensive. Living with verbal abuse requires a hardened shell to deflect each javelin of critical words. Steven also grew up with an unpredictable and critical parent—his father.

Steven, shattered by the death of his brother, was undoubtedly frightened he would lose his mother as well. He seemed to prepare himself for her death by distancing himself from her and protecting his emotions.

I tried to help Tammy understand the importance of dealing with the illness and mortality of our loved ones while communication is possible, so that misunderstandings can be corrected and forgiveness shared. Tammy was able to hear these suggestions and in subsequent appointments, she indicated there was a significant thaw in her relationship with Steven. With his fiancée's help they were spending quality time together. They are three wonderful people who deserve to get love and enjoy one another.

Tammy likes to give Xanax credit for saving her life and enabling her to become independent and productive without experiencing soul crushing panic attacks. She is an example of a patient who used a potentially addictive medicine responsibly, and it is her strength that deserves the credit. I feel Tammy's story is an important one for medical providers to read. Sadly, some patients who could benefit from benzodiazepine medications are being denied them due to the fear of misuse.

What is Agoraphobia and Panic Disorder?

Panic disorder is a type of anxiety disorder in which a sudden attack of fear or anxiety is associated with a long list of symptoms that may appear to be other things.[9] Signs may include:

- palpitations
- pounding heart or accelerated heart rate
- sweating
- trembling or shaking
- shortness of breath or smothering
- feelings of choking
- chest pain or discomfort (the cause of many ER visits, especially with young men)
- nausea or abdominal distress
- feeling dizzy, unsteady, light-headed, or faint
- chills or heat sensations
- numbness or tingling of the fingers and toes
- de-realization (feelings of unreality) or depersonalization (being detached from oneself)
- fear of losing control or "going crazy"
- fear of dying

A full blown panic attack can be terrifying, especially the first time it happens, and panic disorder may be misdiagnosed as other conditions. These patients often go through extensive (and expensive) diagnostic procedures to rule out a medical origin for the symptoms. Tammy underwent cardiac and neurological testing before being diagnosed with panic disorder.

---

9   American Psychiatric Association, *Desk Reference to the Diagnostic Criteria from DSM-5*, (Washington, DC: American Psychiatric Publishing, 2013), 119-120.

The fear of having another panic attack can lead to avoiding the place or activity in which the first one occurred. For many people this means avoiding crowds and even their workplace. In extreme situations, this avoidance can develop into agoraphobia—fear of leaving the home. Tammy was unable to go out unaccompanied and could no longer work at the family restaurant.

People with panic attacks often avoid events and situations that should bring enjoyment. Sometimes taking a benzodiazepine under the tongue 20 minutes before an event can prevent an attack. In some cases just carrying the medication is enough to prevent an attack. Beta blockers normally prescribed for hypertension can reduce the anxiety and potential for a panic attack by decreasing the heart rate—a symptom that often begins with the onset of panic. Combining medication with cognitive behavioral therapy helps people manage their unrealistic fears and distorted thinking, replacing them with more realistic thoughts and the ability to lead happier lives.

What is Xanax?

Xanax belongs to a class of antianxiety medications (benzodiazepines) that can have sedating, anti-convulsive, and muscle-relaxing effects. They differ in speed of onset, which may determine how effectively they prevent a panic attack. Xanax (alprazolam) and lorazepam (Ativan) are used to prevent or cut short panic attacks. Diazepam (valium) and clonazepam (klonopin) have a longer duration of activity and help manage symptoms throughout the day. The short action of Xanax can lead to overuse and abuse, because in just a few hours the body may begin feeling withdrawal sensations that mimic anxiety.

Unfortunately for patients who use these medications responsibly and do not respond fully or at all to other drugs, benzodiazepines have a long history of prescription drug abuse. For that reason, some prescribers are reluctant to order these medications. Tammy is one of many people who tremendously benefitted from a benzodiazepine that allowed her to manage a difficult disorder and lead a fulfilling, productive life.

Chapter 11
Embracing Our Symptoms: What They Teach Us
Helene

WHEN A PERSON enters therapy they usually want to solve a problem, seek advice, feel better, and occasionally, change. I say "occasionally" because people with problems may feel everyone else needs to change.

Some clients are looking for medication to relieve the misery of painful symptoms, such as extreme panic, fear, flashbacks of trauma, obsessive compulsive behaviors, exquisite self-consciousness and social anxiety, confusion, paranoia, auditory hallucinations, depression with suicidal thoughts, or insomnia. But just as physical symptoms like joint pain tell us something in the body needs attention, these mental symptoms alert us to underlying problems.

At times I've felt that giving medication for depression and anxiety to a woman who's in an unhealthy and unsatisfying relationship makes me an enabler of her dysfunction. Because her symptoms are telling her to either leave or work on the relationship, masking them with medication may not be the best answer.

Discomfort may cause us to make needed changes in our lives, and often the worsening of symptoms is a hallmark that change is on the horizon. Women with a history of abuse can learn to use their fearfulness and suspicion to discover red flags in potential partners.

Severely abused people often display or describe a dark side to their natures that frightens them when it emerges. In our work together, a client of mine with multiple personality disorder was gradually able to see how this "evil," dangerous side of her personality kept her alive as a child, and later emerged in adulthood when she felt threatened. The picture book for adults, *Accepting the Troll*

Underneath the Bridge: Overcoming our Self-Doubts,[10] by Terry D. Cooper, helped me show her that when we meet our dark side face to face and embrace and thank it for its protection, that part of us may become more peaceful and less frightening.

Working with victims of abuse opened my eyes to the fact that all of us have various aspects to our personalities. A body of literature explores the shadow self we work hard to ignore. This shadow tends to hold our less positive characteristics, usually the attributes we despise in others. Once we can admit to having the shadow, its unconscious influence is diminished.

As annoying as symptoms may be, sometimes noticing and making friends with them can be more productive than suppressing and ignoring them. We can all learn from our symptoms if we aren't paralyzed by them and at their mercy. The more completely we understand our thinking and what motivates our behavior, the more in charge WE are, not the TROLL.

---

10   Cooper, Terry D. *Accepting the Troll Underneath the Bridge: Overcoming our Self-Doubts*, Wipf & Stock Publishing, 2010.

Chapter 12
Sexual Abuse: From Victim, to Survivor, to Thriver

Patricia

AS IS OFTEN the case when I work with survivors of sexual abuse, they do not enter treatment requesting help with this issue. Rather, it often takes months of treatment for other personal issues, marriage problems, work difficulties, or concerns about children, before the patient discloses sexual abuse. Only after a person believes she can trust the therapist, and feels empathy and concern from the therapist, does the patient begin revealing the "deep, dark secret" she may have been carrying around for decades.

My first impression of Gail was of a depressed woman. She entered my therapy office stooped over and barely making eye contact. She rarely smiled, and although she was well kept, she dressed in a dowdy schoolmarm manner and was overweight. She spoke softly, with few facial expressions.

Gail began therapy saying she had concerns about her only child, a twelve year old daughter who was having health problems. After many medical tests combined with trial and error medications, Gail's only child was diagnosed with juvenile arthritis. This disturbed Gail, who is a highly trained nurse practitioner and realized the diagnosis would be a lifelong sentence for her daughter. Shortly thereafter Gail had to begin administering weekly injections of a potent anti-inflammatory medication to relieve her daughter's pain and suffering.

Gail asked me to see her daughter for a session to determine if she would benefit from counseling. I agreed to do this as an initial consult, but I rarely agree to see two members of a family in therapy at the same time. I believe this could make one or both patients have doubts about confidentiality and they worry about what the other family member is saying. This is especially true for teenagers, who need to feel whatever they share with a therapist will be confidential from their parents. Confidentiality does apply to children and teenagers as well as adults. Psychologists are only mandated to report to parents what we hear in therapy with children if the child or adolescent has threatened to hurt themselves or another person, or they're being hurt by another person.

When I met with Gail's daughter she was a delightful, upbeat twelve year old who said she was happy at school and with friends, and didn't mind her Mom giving her shots. She said, "You know, my mom is a really good nurse!"

As I explored home life a bit further I was surprised to hear Gail's daughter wasn't fond of her father. She said, "He's only into himself."

Gail had never offered anything but positive comments about her husband, to whom she'd been married for twenty years. Only after talking to her daughter did I realize this might be a topic that needed further inquiry and discussion.

At my next session with Gail I told her I thought her daughter was doing fine and didn't need therapy. Gail gave a huge sigh of relief when I told her this, and added, "I would do anything to spare my daughter pain." I followed this information with more questions about Gail's marriage and home life. She said she wasn't ready to talk about this and I told her that was okay. I said, "Therapy is really about what you need, Gail, so during the next session, why don't we discuss what you want to work on in therapy?"

The next session was a doozy! Gail started by saying she had many things to tell me, that she trusted me and wanted to share, but wasn't sure she could do it. She was afraid. When I hear this kind of plea my mind goes to concern for the patient's safety. I think of domestic abuse and/or prior sexual abuse. When I asked if Gail was in danger in her current life in any way, she said, "No, I'm not."

I asked if her husband was physically abusive, and she replied, "No."

I then asked if he was verbally abusive. She paused and with eyes downcast whispered, "Sometimes."

I could barely hear her. I moved closer to make sure I didn't miss her words. She said, "I can't say more."

At this moment, Gail appeared to be in another world and I could see her dissociative state for the first time. I said, "That's enough for today," and turned the topic to more mundane questions about her job and how her daughter was doing. I tried to bring her back to present reality before she left my office.

I knew I must proceed cautiously with Gail. Her resistance was apparent, and I knew from past work with abuse survivors—especially sexual abuse survivors, which is what I suspected Gail needed to talk about—that I must "peel back the onion" layer by layer. When a patient goes into a dissociative state, it's as if they're in a trance or "out of body." They are most likely reliving or protecting themselves from some traumatic event they are re-experiencing.

During the next three years of meeting with Gail on a weekly basis, little by little, she began disclosing one of the most disturbing tales of childhood sexual and physical abuse I had ever heard in my practice. She would describe "out of body" experiences where she left her body and floated in the corner of the room while the sexual abuse occurred. It also became apparent that Gail was in a loveless marriage with a selfish, self-absorbed man. But, thanks to the emotional scars and traumas of her childhood, she didn't believe she deserved anything better in a marriage.

Gail's treatment was especially challenging because she continued having trouble speaking the words of her abuse. A technique that worked with Gail was to have her write down what had happened to her as a child. She'd never spoken of her abuse and found journaling helpful. She wanted me to read out loud what she had written during the session; and with this approach the clinical work of healing began.

My first step was to help Gail realize she was the victim and the abuse perpetrated upon her was not her fault in any way. This is often difficult for victims of sexual abuse to believe. My goal was to help Gail move from victim to a survivor with a voice. I clearly remember one session when I was reading Gail's words about her abuse and she began trembling. I wrapped a blanket that I have in my office around her shoulders and told her, "You are safe." She cried and cried. I think that was a major breakthrough for Gail. Her resistance had melted. She trusted me and knew I cared for her and we were on the same side. We had formed a therapeutic alliance.

After that session Gail began using her own voice to speak of the abuse. She began making direct eye contact with me and opened up about many family of origin secrets and atrocities. She confronted some family members who had abused her. She joined sexual abuse survivor support groups. And she started a sexual harassment forum at the college where she taught. Week by week, month by month, Gail began her journey of healing.

This was a bumpy road, with medications, suicidal ideation, and inpatient hospitalizations. It took three years of intense treatment, but over time Gail began to heal. She no longer was a victim; she no longer was simply a survivor; now she was what I call a thriver.

Gail has gone on to divorce her husband, obtain her doctorate degree in nursing, and see her daughter graduate from college and enter a promising career. In addition Gail made changes in her outward appearance. She cut, colored, and attractively styled her hair. She now walks and exercises daily and has lost weight. Gail buys fashionable, stylish clothing and wears funky jewelry. She smiles and laughs. She began dating, saying she was finally ready for a healthy relationship. She now loves herself and knows she deserves to be loved by a healthy man.

Gail has found her "good man" and is engaged to be married. They take weekly ballroom dancing lessons together. I plan to be at that special wedding to joyfully welcome another new, bright chapter in Gail's life.

Resources:

National Center for Post-Traumatic Stress Disorder, U.S. Department of Veteran's Administration:

1. **Dissociative Subtype of PTSD**: Recent research evaluating the relationship between posttraumatic stress disorder and dissociation has suggested there is a dissociative subtype of PTSD, defined primarily by symptoms of derealization (feeling as if the world is not real). Confrontation with overwhelming experience from which actual escape is not possible, such as childhood abuse, torture, as well as war trauma, challenges the victim to find an escape from the external environment and their internal distress and arousal when no escape is possible. States of depersonalization, dissociation, and derealization provide striking examples of how consciousness can be altered to accommodate an overwhelming experience and allow the person to continue functioning under fierce conditions.

An "out of body" or depersonalization experience occurs when people see themselves observing their own bodies from above. This creates the perception that "this is really not happening to me."

Derealization occurs when people experience the "this is not real; it's just a dream" and creates the perception "this is not really happening to me."

2. **Therapeutic Alliance:** The therapeutic alliance is a component of the therapeutic relationship. The therapeutic or working alliance is defined as the joining of a client's reasonable side with a therapist's working or analyzing side. The bond forms from trust and confidence that the tasks of therapy will bring the client closer to her goals. Research on the therapeutic alliance suggests it is a strong predictor of positive psychotherapy client outcome.

Child Sexual Abuse Statistics:

David Finkelhor, Director of the Crimes Against Children Research Center, www.unh.edu.

- One in five girls and one in ten boys is a victim of sexual abuse;
- In a one year period in United States, 16% of youth ages fourteen to seventeen have been sexually victimized;
- Over the course of a lifetime, 28% of youth ages fourteen to seventeen have been sexually victimized;
- Children are most vulnerable to sexual abuse between the ages of seven and thirteen.

Sexual Abuse Support Groups:

www.rainn.org (Rape, Abuse and Incest National Network)
www.ascasupport.org (Adult Survivors of Child Abuse)
ASCA "Survivor to Thriver Manual"

Chapter 13

A Promise to God:
Surviving Childhood Abuse and Neglect

Patricia

CATHERINE GRACEFULLY WALKED into my office, gently shook my hand, smiled at me, and delicately sat on my office loveseat. She was a sixty-something, stylishly dressed woman in gray slacks and a periwinkle blue V-neck sweater with a simple, elegant cross pendant resting on her clavicle. Her natural white hair was fashioned in a tasteful short haircut that flattered her face.

Upon meeting her, I thought, "What an elegant, beautiful lady." The emphasis was on "lady." She appeared to have all the grace and manners of a woman raised in a refined home with values of culture and civility. When we began our initial session, Catherine started by saying in a delicate, articulate voice, "Oh, my, I've never been to therapy. I really don't know what to expect, but it certainly is a pleasure to meet you, Dr. Martin."

Again, I told myself, "What a refined lady. Working with her is going to be a pleasure." And as the years of therapy went on, I realized my initial impressions of Catherine were correct: she is quite a lady—a woman who molded her own life to create her best possible self. She is her own creation, her own life composition, not the product of a refined, cultured background.

Catherine was the perfect example to me of not judging a book by its cover. Although at seventy-four years of age (she looks fifty-five) she truly is a lovely woman, her graceful countenance belies one of the most abusive backgrounds I've encountered in my thirty years of private practice.

Catherine's story is about a young girl who realized she wanted a better life than the one she was living and through a promise to God made herself into a cultivated, gracious adult. It is a story about courage, conviction, and perseverance;

about staying the course even with great obstacles in your way. It is a story about finding your voice and speaking your truth, be it a fierce roar of "NO!" or a gentle, kind voice of "Oh, my, what a pleasure."

Catherine came to see me at the recommendation of her daughter, whom I had counseled years before. I remembered hearing Catherine's daughter refer to her as "June Cleaver." June was the perfect mother on the 1960's television show "Leave It To Beaver," who always wore pastel dresses cinched at the waist (probably a twenty-four inch waist), a perfect hairdo, and a pearl necklace—and all this was for doing housework. In the kitchen she added an apron to her ensemble and dinner was served promptly at six, with her husband and two sons, Wally and Beaver, spic and span at the dinner table, pleasantly discussing events of the day.

I discovered that June Cleaver was a fairly accurate physical description of Catherine, except Catherine worked full time while raising a son and daughter and was married to a traveling salesman who unbeknownst to her, cheated on her throughout their marriage. Catherine only discovered these infidelities when, after forty-three years of marriage, her husband came home one day and said he wanted a divorce and was going to live with his girlfriend. Now that the children were grown, he no longer wanted the burden of being Catherine's husband.

Catherine was almost numb with shock and wondered how she could survive financially without him. But, because of her loyalty and love for her husband's mother over the years, Catherine was willed half of her mother-in-law's estate, vehemently contested by her ex. Yet Catherine prevailed in court and was awarded her share of her mother-in-law's estate. Catherine was saved by this generosity and able to survive the divorce.

Catherine entered therapy a couple of years after her divorce. She had started dating a man, but was depressed and confused by his negligent and demanding treatment of her. At this point in her life she wanted to know what a healthy relationship looked like, and she asked me to help her learn to tell good men from playboy types. She shyly admitted she had little experience with men and didn't recognize normal behavior in dating.

After Catherine handed me a seven page, hand written, single spaced composition, I realized she had much to tell me about her life—and that her outward appearance was totally different from how she was reared. Catherine was clear that she didn't want to speak of the past, which is why she gave me a written history.

I read through the pages with tears in my eyes, wondering how she ever survived such a sordid past. Obviously she wondered what was normal and healthy because she mostly experienced abnormal and unhealthy during her early life. Her story included being abandoned by her mother at three years of age while her father was away in the service, time in an orphanage, stints in foster homes, sexual and physical abuse by her father, and verbal and physical abuse by a step-mother.

I read in amazement how she fled at age twenty with only the clothes on her back and a small suitcase. When I asked Catherine how she managed through these tortuous times, she calmly looked at me with her big, blue-gray eyes, and calmly said, "I made a promise to God."

"Can you tell me more about that promise?" I asked.

Catherine said, "I prayed and prayed to find a way out of that terrible house. Sometimes I would pretend the windows of the garages in the alley were the Stations of the Cross and prayed to God to save me. I vowed if He would help me get out of that hell I would lead a better, upstanding life. I would make up for the sins of my parents and I would lead a life worthy of God's love."

She went on to say, "My prayers were answered in the form of kind, good people who helped show me a different way over my childhood years; and I kept my promise to God."

Catherine has given me permission to share excerpts from the document she wrote about her life. I share her memories with you to let you know that, in spite of horrific events, the human spirit can endure and triumph and a voice can be found to say, "No! No more!"

Catherine's Story

I was born in 1941 and my father went to war. My mother had parties with service men. I remember standing up in a crib and crying because I was alone. My aunts told me neighbors would call and tell them my mother had left me alone at night. She had one of her soldiers bring me to my paternal grandparents' house when I was three years old. I could not stay there because my grandmother was paralyzed and my father could not care for me as a veteran with bad PTSD and alcoholism.

I was then sent to an orphanage. I remember gagging on bread and milk the nuns were feeding me. My father was told to find me a home with a family, because I was not doing well and I had impetigo.

I was sent to live with a foster family when I was four. They had a big house in the country, a son away in the Marine Corps, and five daughters. They also had two other children boarding with them. I slept in a big bed with the two youngest daughters. We would say our prayers at night with the mother, and she would only kiss her two daughters goodnight, not me. Somehow I learned it was better to not look for attention because that would annoy them. I lived in foster care for four years until I was eight years old.

My father's sister bought a house and said I could live with her and my uncle and two younger boy cousins. I once heard my aunt tell my other aunt that I would be like my mother. (I do not know why she said this.) But, I decided to find out what my mother liked and didn't like and I would choose the opposite.

Later that year my father married my stepmother and I left my aunt's house and moved to the city and a three room apartment. The entire street was apartments from first to third floor. We lived on the first floor. We had an alley for the backyard. It was quite different from the country. I used to cry when I saw roaches or found bed bugs in my sheets. I had to make a lot of noise when I emptied the trash because of rats. I felt so embarrassed because my father swore a lot and made a lot of noise. I remember standing on my studio couch where I slept in the living room and crying and pleading to the police not to take my father away. The neighbors called the police when my father got too drunk and threw things around.

When I was nine, my step-mother went into the hospital to have her first child. It was during her time away that my father raped me three times while my step-mother was in the hospital. He told me it was our secret and that it was a father's job to teach his daughter how babies were made. I remember the drool coming from his mouth made me sick. I wanted to tell my friend, but was afraid that this was not something other fathers did to their daughters, and I would be ashamed and embarrassed and ridiculed. So I kept it a secret, but I would never allow myself to be alone with my father.

When my step-mother had more children I would ask that we go to the foster family's home where I had lived as a young child. I was allowed to go if I brought my younger brother and sister and cared for them. I was afraid of my father and would lock my door when he was around and drunk.

When I was nine, I was expected to care for the first child, and then when my sister was born I was to care for her in the afternoon. My friends got used to me having my brother and sister with me all the time. When I was fourteen the third child was born and my step-mother got a night time job and I was to get supper and watch the three kids every day after school.

In high school I was elected secretary of the high school class and I would have to go out on Wednesday nights. My girlfriend's mother offered to babysit for me, but my step-mother said no. There were many things I wanted to do, but was told I couldn't because I had to babysit.

The landlords lived upstairs in the two-family house where we later lived. There was too much noise from my house, so we were evicted. My father said it was my fault because I didn't keep the kids quiet. The landlord's wife told me differently. She was nice and would help me with sewing questions. When we moved again, we lived in veteran's housing.

My school and friends were the best part of my life. I found it hard to concentrate on studies with all the noise and confusion in my house. I started at the hospital nursing program, but could not keep up with the work. My father was very disappointed in me. I started working at nineteen at a manufacturing company. It was worse at home now, as my step-mother had another baby and was beginning to have bipolar episodes. My father wanted me to stay home and take care of the house and let my step-mother work. She needed to get out and she would make more money.

I said, "No!" Shortly after that, at supper time my father was drinking and hollering at the table. I couldn't stand it anymore. I just got up, went into my bedroom, packed my suitcase, and said I was leaving. My father said he would help me and took my suitcase and threw it on the lawn. I left the house and started to cry. I stopped at my best girlfriend's house and was asked to stay overnight. The next day at work one of my friends said the lady who owned her boarding house had an extra room to rent. And that is where I lived until I met my husband two years later. The lady at the boarding house was a single woman who was very kind and cooked meals for my friend and me. I was happy there.

With little experience in dating, Catherine entered marriage as a virgin. Her promise to God included remaining chaste until she was married. Unfortunately she married a man who had played the field and was not sexually interested in her; rather he thought she would be a good mother to their children. Not long after they married, Catherine remembers her husband saying to her, "I wish I had married a whore; you just lie there."

She said she was humiliated and embarrassed by this. Catherine told me, "This killed the depths of me."

Even though her husband was a selfish, philandering man, Catherine was close to her in-law parents. They loved her and thought she was the best thing that ever happened to their playboy, only son. Catherine cared for her mother-in-law, who lived nearby, until her death at ninety years of age. Catherine was also a wonderful mother to her two children, and now to her three grandchildren. She also has maintained a relationship with her four step-siblings for whom she cared during most of her childhood. She has become the mother who hosts them for holidays and is their shoulder to cry on when things don't go well, or their health care proxy when they have emotional/psychological problems and health issues.

Catherine is a kind, refined, beautiful woman; a woman who never had maternal or paternal love herself, yet by the grace of God and utter determination has become one of the best mothers I've ever met.

During the course of our therapy she realized she was currently in a sexually and emotionally abusive dating relationship. The man she was dating would criticize her decisions and choices, ignore her when in the presence of other women, and force her to do things sexually she was not comfortable doing. She realized she was just fine without a man in her life, and broke up with him. Catherine has decided she is no longer looking for, nor does she need, a man to be complete. She is content being a mother and grandmother and having many friends. She knits and tap dances with friends and has a book club, garden club, and hiking club with whom she socializes. Just the other day she brought me a frame with a quote inside that reminded her of her journey in therapy. It reads, "Falling down is part of life. Getting back up is living." When Catherine dies, she wants to be cremated and buried with flowers above her grave; no headstone and not in a cemetery near anyone. She calmly states, "I came in alone and will go out alone." She has come to peace.

Chapter 14
Sobriety, Serenity, and Goody Bags:
Overcoming Alcoholism

Patricia

MANY PATIENTS WHO enter therapy for depression, anxiety, or mood swings suffer from some kind of underlying substance abuse. Until the substance abuse problem is addressed in therapy it is impossible to focus on other problem areas, such as grief, sexual abuse, depression, or anxiety. Alcohol is often the self-medicating drug of choice to numb patients' negative feelings and to mask other problems.

For Lori, the never ending carousel of one-night stands with both male and female partners was beginning to wear thin. She entered my therapy office with a veneer of confidence and calm that soon evaporated when our conversation moved from superficial introductions to the meaty matters of relationships and alcohol use.

Lori was in a ten year live-in relationship with a coworker from the school where she taught. During her relationship with her partner she had been continually unfaithful, cheating recklessly with other coworkers and subordinates. She was in a cycle of infidelity, being scolded, repenting, and cheating again. Each of these incidents involved the abuse of alcohol. The topic of alcohol came up in nearly every session. Lori was miserable and she drank. Her drink of choice was straight up vodka martinis, which she lapped down by the pint nearly every night. She was sick and tired of this life-style.

Her family history was replete with alcoholism—her father, uncle, and brother were chronic alcoholics. She was the only female left in a household with three men (her father and two brothers) when her mother died of multiple sclerosis when Lori was twelve. She was reluctant to share her story of sexual and physical abuse, but in time was able to unload this psychic baggage. Her sexual abuse occurred early in life by an uncle while his wife was babysitting her. The physical abuse occurred at the hands of her father. Her alcoholism kicked into high gear after she left the family home and started college.

Lori was a functional alcoholic who could go to work, put in a full day of teaching and business meetings, and then head to the bars to socialize with fellow coworkers. She tried to quit drinking on several occasions, but was always lured back into the habit by her buddies, including her partner, who would jest that Lori was no more an alcoholic than any of them. They would continue repeating "You're just a social drinker," to the point that Lori believed them. Of course her friends didn't think they had a drinking problem either, as they pounded down their fourth martini and numerous Jello shots.

Lori began to realize over the course of therapy that her partner was abusive in a passive aggressive way, saying she loved Lori, yet constantly criticizing her. Lori wanted to leave her partner but was convinced she couldn't manage on her own—a belief her partner continued to reinforce with Lori after every drinking binge. Lori's partner, who was ten years her senior, was one in a string of older women with whom Lori had been involved. She seemed unaware of this repeated dynamic of trying to find a replacement for her mother, but she was growing tired of these controlling mother figures in her life.

One Monday night I heard my pager going off at about 10 p.m. I was home with my husband and four children. We had just finished our nightly routine of getting the children to bed and were getting to other tasks on our endless daily chore list. I was placing candy and toy items in goody bags for school the next day to celebrate my eight year old daughter's birthday. Each bag contained Smarties, Tootsie Rolls, Blow Pops, and stickers—a moment I'll never forget. I was trying to focus on putting the right amount in each bag, becoming more and more tired, when the buzz of the pager startled me to alertness.

I dialed the number on the pager and was greeted by "Hi, Pat," barely audible and very slurred and incoherent.

I wasn't sure if I was too tired to hear correctly or we had a bad connection, but I had the presence of mind to ask "Who is this?"

The caller mumbled her name, but I couldn't make out the words. What I did hear was sobbing and long pauses. Finally, I understood the word "Lori."

I asked if she'd been drinking, to which she replied, "Yes."

Then I asked where she was. No reply. She kept crying, saying she missed her mom (this was the day after Mother's Day). She slurred, "I want to die and be with my mother," something I had never heard before from Lori.

I again asked where she was and how much had she drunk. She said a quart of vodka and added she'd also taken some Ativan. I kept the best soothing voice going that I could muster and kept trying to get her location so I could send help. She refused to cooperate. The long pauses seemed to go on forever, a silence I can hear to this day.

Finally, she asked me, "Whatcha doin' Pat?"

I answered, "I'm making goody bags for my daughter's birthday party."

She garbled, "Whaaat are goody bags?"

I remember thinking how sad that she didn't know, realizing she most likely never had a birthday party with goody bags due to her mother's chronic invalid state and her dad's alcoholism. I tried to explain about goody bags. As I described every item in the bag, I could tell she was listening on the other end of the phone.

"Ohh….that is so nice…..that is sooo nice," was the slurred response.

I told her again that I wanted to help her and she would be okay. The goody bags seemed to snap Lori out of her stupor and she told me the address where she was. I kept her on the line while I called the local police using my mobile phone. They arrived at Lori's address within minutes and she was rushed to the hospital to have her stomach pumped, IV's administered, and vital signs monitored. Thankfully, she survived.

I saw her the next day and we had an in depth talk about how difficult all Mother's Days were for her. She said hearing me talk about goody bags and my love for my children is what saved her. It gave her hope that the world was not an awful place.

That was the beginning, day one, of Lori's sobriety. She is now seventeen years sober and an active member of Alcoholics Anonymous. That day was also the start of grief work in therapy and the end of her choosing and staying in unhealthy relationships.

I like to use a metaphor in therapy about patience and perseverance related to psychological change and growth: "The Miracle of the Chinese Bamboo Tree." Lori wanted me to share this story, as she says it has helped her throughout her sobriety and the challenges in her life. This story comes from Steven Covey's book *The Seven Habits of Highly Effective Families*.[11]

After the seed for this amazing tree is planted, you see nothing, absolutely nothing, for four years except for a tiny shoot coming out of a bulb. During those four years, all the growth is underground in a massive, fibrous root structure that spreads deep and wide in the earth. But then, in the fifth year, the Chinese bamboo tree grows up to eighty feet.

Just like the bamboo tree, seventeen years after the goody bag night, Lori is a contented, successful school administrator who has thousands of children under her care. During her first five years of sobriety she didn't get involved in any personal

---

11   Covey, Steven. *The Seven Habits of Highly Effective Families,* Boca Raton: Premier Publishing Company, 1997, The Miracle of the Chinese Bamboo Tree. p. 22-23.

sexual relationships. She focused on her AA program and finished her doctorate in education. She is now in an eleven year relationship with a loving, even tempered, healthy, same-aged partner and is happy most days and able to manage the difficult times with her sobriety.

Lori has been an inspiration to me in her dogged, tenacious therapeutic work, her commitment to the AA program, and her devotion to her school family and friend family. She has taught me that sobriety allows one to face the losses of life head on and grab onto the serenity and joy that exist in life. She is a true treasure to so many people, and I will forever be grateful she reached out to me on that May night seventeen years ago.

Another valuable lesson from this story is that life preservers come in all shapes and sizes—in this case, that of a goody bag. What we think is simple and mundane may be the exact statement or life-saving line that can help someone in distress.

Data on Alcoholism:

- National Institute on Alcohol Abuse and Alcoholism (www.niaaa.nih.gov)

In the US about eighteen million people have Alcohol Use Disorder (AUD) be it alcohol dependence or alcohol abuse

- Alcohol use disorder is considered by the NIAAA for men: four + drinks a day or fourteen+ drinks a week; for women: three + drinks a day or seven + drinks a week

www.aa.org;
www.12step.org;
http://healthpsych.psy.vanderbilt.edu/12step.htm.

- Alcoholics Anonymous was created by Bill Wilson and Dr. Bob Smith in 1930s and the book *Alcoholics Anonymous* was published in 1939 to outline the twelve step program and their mission. Now, AA is all over the world with greater than 97,000 groups; and over two million members.

2007 survey of AA's effectiveness:

- 33% of members were sober over ten years.
- 12% of members were sober five to ten years
- 24% of members were sober one to five years
- 31% of members were sober less than one year.
- Percentage of Women in AA 33%; Percentage of Men in AA 67%

The Serenity Prayer

God grant me the serenity to accept the things I cannot change;
Courage to change the things I can;
And wisdom to know the difference.
Living one day at a time;
Enjoying one moment at a time;
Accepting hardships as the pathway to peace;
Taking as He did, this sinful world
As it is, not as I would have it;
Trusting that He will make all things right
If I surrender to His Will;
That I may be reasonably happy in this life
And supremely happy with Him
Forever in the next.
Amen

Movies about Sobriety: *Clean and Sober; Days of Wine and Roses; 28 Days.*
Song: *Better Than I Used to Be,* by Tim McGraw.

Chapter Fifteen
Self Esteem and the Single Mother: I Deserve Better
Patricia

"AS THE TWIG IS BENT, so grows the tree."

Without positive influences, it's difficult to bend one's life in a positive direction. Growing up in poverty can place a person in a negative cycle that's difficult to escape. But every now and then I meet someone in therapy who managed to overcome the bad influences of her past and live differently than her parents and family. Such was my client, Maria—a true inspiration in her commitment to a better life for herself, her brother and sister, and most importantly her daughter.

Maria came to therapy as a recent college graduate, frustrated by a relationship with her college boyfriend. She wanted a committed fiancé who was interested in having a family, complete with the proverbial white picket fence and all the trimmings. As she told me her story I understood why she craved a safe, solid family life.

Maria grew up in the Bronx in New York City in a family that originated in Puerto Rico. Her memories of childhood included rarely seeing her father, who worked repairing heating units. He also had a second job: dealing drugs from their apartment. She remembers having to hide when he brought in customers to buy drugs. She was constantly afraid their home would be raided by the police and her father hauled off to jail. After several years and two other children, Maria's mother decided to leave her father. She moved herself and the children to Cape Cod, Massachusetts—a huge contrast to the streets and tenements of the Bronx.

As the only child of color in her entire school, Maria was frequently asked about her nationality, but no one understood what she meant when she said Puerto Rican. While living with her single mother, Maria learned about being on welfare. Her father was mostly negligent in paying child support and her mother needed assistance to keep Maria and her younger brother and sister fed and a roof over their heads. Neither of her parents had completed high school, let alone considered a college education. Still Maria wanted something better in life, and she set out to find it.

Through a program at her high school she was selected for a special mentoring group. Largely because of this program and her committed mentor, Maria found a way out of poverty. She was guided throughout her high school years to maintain a high grade point average and challenge herself with honors level courses. A guidance teacher helped Maria apply to colleges and find loans for school. When the time came to enter college, Maria worried about leaving her mother who was always having medical concerns. But mentors encouraged her to take the plunge—and thus began the journey to a better life for herself and her family.

Her college years included working part time jobs while studying to become a social worker. At times she almost had to drop out due to lack of money for books or registration. Again, the mentor program from high school came to the rescue by providing financial assistance. While in college she encouraged her younger brother to join the same mentor program in high school. With this support he was able to attend college like his older sister. Throughout college Maria continued worrying about her mother's welfare, both health-wise and financially. Her father had little to do with her during those years.

Maria's first job after college was as a caseworker for a human services agency. Her fluency in Spanish proved a valuable asset and her direct, no nonsense approach was an effective intervention strategy for thousands of families during her tenure at the department. Maria worked a second evening job a few times a week as a crisis hot line worker. Her goal was to save enough money to buy her own home.

Maria's social life wasn't as successful and productive as her work life. She dated several men over the years, finding repeated disappointments with the men she met. All of them seemed to be interested in a sexual relationship, but not a commitment. She wondered if she'd every find the right man to marry and start a family. During her early thirties she began dating a security guard. After several months they moved in together, and within a year Maria became pregnant. Her boyfriend wasn't thrilled, but they decided to keep the baby and make a go of it as a committed couple.

Maria believed this was the beginning of her dream life. Before the baby was born they bought a house together and set up for the family that would soon begin. Maria was thrilled to become a mother and thought in time her boyfriend would warm to the concept of fatherhood. Instead, he began distancing himself more and more from her, frequently staying away from home taking more overtime jobs. She tried to make their relationship work, even entering couples therapy for six months.

As their baby moved into the toddler stage, Maria saw her boyfriend take a greater interest in his daughter. She was happy and thought he might be evolving toward getting married. She waited and hoped for almost a year, then finally explored the topic of marriage with him. He told her he had absolutely no interest in marrying her.

Maria was devastated, but pulled herself together and decided to leave the relationship. Her statement to me was, "I deserve better! I want a man who loves me enough to marry me, and if he doesn't feel that way then I'm better on my own."

She left and bought her own house, which she lovingly rehabbed and made into a home for herself and her daughter. Now, a year later, she has enrolled in a master's program to enhance her career and future. She is a wonderful mother who tries to make sure her daughter gets the best educational opportunities and extracurricular activities. She takes her daughter to the theater, sports and dancing, and they travel around the country together. She wants to give her daughter every opportunity she missed as a child.

Maria doesn't know if a husband is in her future, but that isn't the most important thing in her life. She broke the cycle of poverty for herself and her siblings through her determination, hard work, and willingness to pursue an education and dream of a better life. Maria asked me to include her thoughts about "A Better Life."

I think people's biggest mistake is living in the past and not even being aware of it. People say, "This is me, and don't try to change me."

The past is the past and does not exist anymore.

Here's the thing; no one can change you, but if you want to be a better person and let go of the past, you must believe in God and believe in yourself.

Open your heart and mind to see the hurt, sadness, and pain you cause others who care for and love you. Be open to seeing where people hold you in their lives and do not let your blindness to resist change or push others away.

Change brings bigger and better things into your life. The world changes daily. The circumstances in your life change, but are you willing to change, evolve, and be better, or do you repeat the same cycle over and over?

To repeat is easy, but to change means making an effort to be committed, to be motivated, and to love yourself fully and believe that a higher power is looking out for you. Then you can say "I am blessed!"

Resources:

www.cafemom.com/single-mom
www.singlemotheerguide.com
www.SPAOA,org
www.singleparents.about.com

Statistics on Single Mother's in USA
From the 2013 census in USA:

- About four out of ten children were born to unwed mothers.
- Nearly two-thirds are born to mothers under the age of thirty.
- Out of twelve million single parent families, more than 80% are headed by single mothers.
- Around 45% of single mothers have never been married, and 55% are either divorced, separated, or widowed. Half of these mothers have one child, while 30% have two children.
- About two thirds of single mothers are White, one third Black, one quarter Hispanic.
- One quarter of single mothers have a college degree; one sixth have not completed high school.
- The median income for families led by a single mother in 2012 was $25,493, one third the median for married couple families ($81,455).
- Only one third of single mothers receive any child support, and the average amount these mothers receive is about $400 a month.

Chapter 16
How Does Therapy Help?
Patricia

AFTER READING THE first fifteen chapters of this book you may be asking yourself, "Exactly how does going to a therapist and doing psychotherapy help a person?"

In some ways the workings of therapy are a mystery and an art. Why is therapy so effective for one client and not another? Is success based on a therapist's individual skill, or is it the willingness and motivation of the patient who comes to therapy?

I believe it's a combination of the two. A therapist who is empathic and caring, with the necessary clinical skills, is likely to provide a safe environment where clients feel secure in sharing their inner thoughts and feelings, as well as hearing a different point of view and listening to counsel on how to live healthier lives. I find therapy works when my client and I have a mutual respect for each other, combined with willingness to change.

This is the **HOW** of living life and doing therapy: **H**onest, **O**pen and **W**illing.

Many people are curious about what actually transpires in the psychotherapist's office during the therapy hour. A 2004 Harris poll determined about 27% of people in the United States have entered a psychotherapist's office at one time or another in their lives. Most are women—about 63% of the total 59 million. Eighty percent of those who received treatment found it effective.[12]

As a psychologist in private practice for over 30 years, I venture to say that every person who walks into my office leaves with their own unique therapy

---

12 Poll, Harris, 2004, "Mental Health Goes Mainstream", *www.consumer.healthday. com.*

experience. Because each person is unique I tailor my therapeutic approach to meet the specific needs and issues of every client.

As a Ph.D. clinical psychologist I was trained in multiple theoretical and treatment modalities during seven years of graduate study. Theoretical approaches included psychodynamic, existential, interpersonal, humanistic, behavioral, cognitive-behavioral, narrative and constructivist, to name a few. A theoretical approach can serve as a framework to help the clinician with her therapeutic work, but a theory does not describe reality or truth—it represents the ever-evolving insight derived from observation and creation. My theoretical orientation is eclectic, in that I'm influenced by existential therapists such as Frankel and Yalom, as well as the cognitive behavioral work of Beck and Ellis, and the narrative constructivist therapeutic models of Hoyt and Neimeyer.

I begin each therapy encounter with these theoretical frameworks in mind, but my actual therapeutic work is primarily relationship driven and unique to the individual clients who enter my office. A recent book by Jonathan Engel, *American Therapy: the Rise of Psychotherapy in the United States,*[13] reviews theoretical approaches over the past 60 years. His conclusion is that in order to be an effective therapist one must draw on the best of these multiple theories. And most importantly, what distinguishes the effective therapist more than training, philosophy, theory, or technique, is the capacity of the therapist to create warmth, empathy, and rapport between herself and the client.

I've always believed my decision to become a psychologist was following a calling rather than choosing a career path. I was fortunate to find a profession that lets me feel fulfilled on a daily basis. My work allows me to transcend my personal issues and focus on the needs and growth of others. Watching and being part of the transformation of another human being's life is an extraordinary privilege. My work gives me the opportunity every day to be intellectually challenged and creatively inspired to find solutions to individual difficulties and recognize problems in the human condition. Practicing therapy impacts my own life. Therapy is a two-way street wherein I learn from my client's life stories, and ideally I move and shape clients with my therapeutic interventions.

What actually happens in therapy is unique to every clinician and every patient. However, I hope each person who enters psychotherapy is able to feel safe and trust the therapist. Each client should feel comfortable to say anything and believe it will be kept in confidence. The ethics of a psychologist are that we can only break confidentiality if we believe the client is at risk of hurting herself or someone else. Other than that, any discussion of our psychotherapy requires written consent from the patient to share with anyone. We are the "cradlers of secrets" according to Irvin Yalom, in his 2001 book, The *Gift of*

---

13   Engle, Jonathan, *American Therapy: the Rise of Psychotherapy in the United States*, Gotham, 2009.

Therapy: Reflections on Being a Therapist.[14] We are honored and privileged to be entrusted with the intimate life stories shared in therapy.

What brings people to psychotherapy? The reasons people enter therapy are as diverse and unique as each therapeutic encounter. I tell clients my approach is to focus on current behaviors that are causing them problems in their lives and then get a historical perspective as needed to help assess the current situation. I let my clients know I am a directive therapist, which means I will give them my thoughts and advice as I think appropriate during the course of therapy. I let them know they are very much part of the process and I want them to tell me if we've missed topics they would like to address. I also will let them know if I detect issues or areas I think we need to discuss. This is their therapy—a chance to talk about their lives, address the things they need to share, and explore avenues that will help them move forward in a more effective way.

The goal of therapy is to identify and remove obstacles that are blocking a client's potential for growth. My job is to help each client better understand and value herself. I like each client to understand her life story so far, and then guide her in putting together a future life story that gives more of what she wants out of life. I work to try to enhance and optimize the choices my clients make in life, based on each person's unique abilities, talents and resources.

I try to move away from pathologizing the person and more into reframing each life as filled with resources and possibilities. We take on the joint work of setting therapeutic goals related to each person's life, including work, friends, personal relationships, family and the community. This therapy belongs to the client and my job is to help each person realize personal autonomy. Each of us holds the key to our own happiness and contentment; my job is to help search for these keys and unlock their full potential as human beings.

Although I'm available for patients as long as they need me, with each person I hope to be out of a job at some point. Rather than termination of therapy, I like to view this as commencement or graduation from therapy. I feel proud to see clients go into the world with new skill sets and inner wisdom discovered on the therapeutic journey. We are fellow travelers.

---

14   Yalom, Irvin, *The Gift of Therapy: Reflections on being a Psychotherapist*, Piatkus Books, 2003.

Stories of Loss

Chapter 17
The Death of a Child: A Loss No Mother Should Bear
Patricia

THERE ARE THE times when I open my office door, see my new client in the waiting room, and immediately know I'm in for a difficult journey. It was such a day in May when I introduced myself to a grim faced couple with tear stained faces looking up at me from their chairs in the waiting area. As they entered my office and took their seats across from me I noted the woman sat alone on the loveseat and the man sat parallel to me in a stuffed chair. She was dressed in black and he wore a blue polo shirt with khaki pants. She was a fifty-something, stern faced, medium height woman with a short crop of dark hair and an olive skin tone. He had a fair complexion, blondish-gray hair, and was tall, I guessed about six foot four inches. While looking at them at a closer range than my previous glimpse in the waiting room, I realized he was the one crying and puffy eyed, while she was dry-eyed, somber, and serious looking. I sensed deep in my bones that she was angry. Very angry.

As a therapist you often do not know beforehand what brings a couple to see you. Frequently when I schedule an appointment the new client wants to wait until the session to give an overview of the problem. When a couple comes for therapy, it could be their marriage is breaking apart due to an affair; or perhaps they're having trouble communicating, they have problems with a child, a job loss, or a recently diagnosed illness. The worst scenario is when a couple is looking for counsel following the death of a child. Such was the case with Mary Anne and Steven; they were seeking therapy two months after the death of their twenty-nine year old son, killed by a drunk driver.

The mother, Mary Anne, told the story of how her only son was killed in a friend's driveway while on a visit to congratulate him on his recent engagement.

She told me he was home from Boston for the weekend to be measured for a tuxedo for his only sister's wedding, which was to be in June. The bereaved mother went on to say life was so good for them; she was getting ready to retire from teaching and her daughter, a physician, had started a practice in Maine and was getting married. The son was an engineer in Boston who was coming home not only to be measured for the tuxedo, but also to buy an engagement ring for his girlfriend. He planned to propose to her on the Fourth of July.

They were happy and she was thrilled to be a mother to such wonderful children. Now tragedy had struck and their lives were forever changed. Mary Anne described her life as a living hell. There are truly no words to respond to such a situation, except to nod and agree how terrible this must be for them.

As Mary Anne related her story I had an eerie feeling I knew it already, from a rare occasion when I watched the local evening news. I remember a crying sister being interviewed about the senseless death of her brother. I asked Mary Anne if her son's name was Robert, and she looked at me with shock in her eyes, and said, "Yes. How do you know this?"

I told her I rarely watch the news, preferring to read newspapers, but for whatever reason one night two months earlier I had it on and was moved to tears after hearing the sister tell her version of what happened. I don't know why I remembered her son's name, perhaps because it's the name of my youngest brother.

After I shared this information, Mary Anne looked straight into my eyes, and with great sadness, yet relief, said, "I am supposed to be here with you."

I had the exact same feeling, and so our therapy began.

After two sessions Steven no longer felt he needed therapy because he was trying to get on with his life. Although he cried daily and terribly missed his son, he didn't think he needed to talk more about it. I understand this is true for many people, so I graciously accepted, letting him know he was welcome to come back whenever he felt a need.

Mary Anne quickly piped up that she needed and wanted to continue therapy. In contrast to her husband, she did not want to "get on with life" and its mundane tasks of shopping or visiting with friends. She felt dead inside and did not want to be part of the outside world. She wanted me to help her through the difficult year ahead, which was going to include a delayed wedding for her daughter as well as preparation for a trial related to her son's killing. I agreed to be there for her as long as she needed me. She nodded with a content resignation that this might be a long haul.

The third session was the beginning of the work Mary Anne would shoulder for the next two and a half years in preparation for her son's "murder" trial. She wanted to do whatever she could to make sure the drunk driver who killed her son received adequate punishment for his crime. She said, "My son's death has to mean something."

As I came to know Mary Anne I realized her stern, put-together exterior belied the true warm, gentle woman underneath. She was sixty at the time of Robert's death and had decided to retire from teaching math in an urban junior high school. Her style of teaching matched her controlled demeanor. She was no-nonsense in her approach, and as a result she commanded the classroom and effectively taught the students. In order to totally not be at sea in September, she chose to volunteer two days a week to tutor in math and help students who were failing the state comprehensive exams. She said this was good for her because when in the classroom with these sixth and seventh graders she was no longer the grieving mother, but instead the math tutor. Her first smiles began to reappear in the classroom setting.

Mary Anne had chosen, perhaps because of her Italian Catholic heritage, to wear black for a solid year of mourning. She kept herself up with manicures and stylish haircuts, but did not deviate from all black clothing for a full year.

That year included the planning and carrying out of her daughter's delayed bridal shower and wedding. Ironically, on the wedding day in October in New England, a freakish snow storm toppled many leaf laden trees and most of us were without electrical power for a week. Mary Anne just rolled with it, saying the wedding went on without a hitch. She said nothing was difficult to handle when compared to the death of her son. In many ways she did all she could to try and appear happy for her daughter, but she would admit to me it all felt a bit robotic due to her state of grieving. But she carried on as the Mother of the Bride and tried to make the day happy for her daughter.

Other events of the year Mary Anne had to endure were cleaning out and selling her son's condo, getting through Fourth of July—the day Robert was going to propose to his girlfriend—ordering a headstone, and creating a scholarship for future engineering students at her son's high school.

Her final task was preparing for the trial. She described this as like running a marathon with no end. The ordeal of over twenty court appearances and numerous delays, added to the grieving year and stress. A mistrial was called due to inadmissible evidence of the defendant's prior cocaine possession, which was inadvertently heard by the jury on a police video. Ironically, this mistrial was declared two years to the day her son was struck by the car driven by the defendant. Fortunately a new trial was ordered and scheduled for three months later with a new jury and an additional assistant district attorney. In total, two years and four months passed before the trial actually began.

In the meantime Mary Anne stayed busy doing what she could to change laws in the state of Massachusetts to lengthen the sentencing time for drug/alcohol related vehicular homicide. She was shocked to learn the average jail sentence was just two years for murdering someone with a car while drunk. It seemed absurd to see sentences of twenty and thirty years for offenses such as drug distribution or child molestation, with as little as a year for vehicular homicide. Not that she felt the other sentences weren't fair or that she didn't feel compassion for those victims; she was angry and "pissed off" at the injustice related to murder at the hands of a drunk driver. Other murderers were put away for life; and her son was just as dead as someone stabbed or shot. She was livid. She channeled her anger into appearing at the State House to file State Bill #3768 requesting longer sentences for vehicular homicide related to drunk driving. In her message she asked the state senate, "What would be enough jail time if this was your child?" With tenacity and directness this grieving mother determined to give meaning and purpose to her son's death.

During the months before the trial Mary Anne worked on a victim impact statement that would be read in the courtroom prior to sentencing by the judge. The family also decided to have a trial by jury of peers rather than solely with a judge. Preparation for the trial included machinations by the defense attorney to get the breathalyzer results dismissed as a false reading. The false reading concept was proposed because the defendant who had a gastric bypass was said to have a "burp" read rather than a "breath" read, and therefore the results were inaccurate.

The family went through a difficult time waiting for the judge's decision regarding admissible evidence of the breathalyzer results, which showed a blood alcohol level reading of .19, twice the legal limit of .08. In the meantime, Mary Anne and her husband researched extensive information on gastric bypass and the effects of intoxication. If need be, they would have hired an expert witness to testify. Fortunately the judge denied the defense attorney's request and the breathalyzer results were admitted.

The time had come to finish Mary Anne's victim impact statement. She wanted to make it a true tribute to her son, to do his death justice. I was there for support, but Mary Anne knew what she wanted to say. She was hitting the hellish "heartbreak hill" of her personal marathon, and she was ready. Mary Anne had doggedly pursued her training and the impact statement was read to the judge.

On September 26, 2013, the defendant was found guilty by a jury of peers and sentenced to a five to seven year state prison term on a vehicular homicide charge for the death of Robert in May, 2011. Even though this seems inadequate, it was one of the most extensive sentences ordered in Massachusetts for that crime. Mary Anne was relieved and content with the decision. She had done her son justice. With her permission I share her victim impact statement:

Thank you, Judge, for allowing me to speak and inform you how the senseless death of my son, Robert, has affected me. I am Mary Anne, and on the evening of May 15, 2011 my world was shattered.

Earlier in the evening my husband Steven and I met Robert at a local restaurant for dinner. We talked of many things, as this was an exciting time in all our lives. Robert returned to visit from his home in Boston to be measured for a tux. He was to be an honor attendant in his sister Jane's June wedding. He was also home so I could accompany him to purchase an engagement ring he designed for his beloved Christina. He planned to propose to her on July 4, 2011. A few days earlier, they had signed documents to purchase a two family home in Hingham as an investment and a love nest. His written list of eleven 2011 goals, which we found upon emptying his condominium, were coming to fruition, one by one.

After dinner, he stopped by his friend John's parents' home to congratulate John on his recent engagement. Around 10:20, John called and told us to go to Baystate Medical Center as there had been an accident. While Steven drove us there, I said numerous Hail Mary's. I tried not to think about what possibly could have happened, but tried to concentrate on my prayers. After waiting a while in the emergency room, we were brought into the trauma room. Robert was lying on a bed. His eyes were closed. He was not conscious. Blood was dripping out of his ear. He did not move. As more tests were completed, the neurologist brought us into a separate, quiet room and our nightmare became worse. He asked us how old Robert was. I told him he was twenty-nine. He cried as he told us there was nothing he could do. What did that mean? It simply did not register.

Robert was moved to the ICU where the living wake began. His family surrounded him. Many friends from his hometown and others from the Boston area camped out in the waiting room. They came to urge him in his recovery, talking to him, holding his hand, singing to him. Little did they know, nothing could be done, except to wait.

What were we waiting for? It still was not making sense to me. Ultimately, we were waiting for his death. Can you possibly imagine what it is like to wait for your child's unnecessary death? Just a few short hours before we were celebrating all the good things life had to offer. Now we waited for him to die.

Robert was a registered organ donor. A doctor spoke to us about fulfilling his wishes. Can any parent find it acceptable to slice up their child and give away the parts that keep them alive? It was impossible to think about, but we conceded to his choice.

On May 16, 2011 at 8:41p.m., my beautiful son's life ended. In order for his organs to be harvested, machines continued his bodily functions. After numerous tears, kisses and hugs, we reached our parting moment. The final time I saw breath rising from Robert's chest, even though it was mechanically accomplished, was as the medical team of doctors and nurses wheeled him into a cold, stainless steel elevator. Then the doors closed. Knowing that his body was to be carved and pieces sent to various locations haunts me to this day. Would you want this as the parting memory of your son?

His organs saved six people.

How has Robert's senseless death impacted me? I could tell you about all the life events that will not be: the marriage, the grandchildren, the birthdays, holidays, the many years I will not have my beloved Robert to hug and kiss me. But I am sure you have heard these things before. The impact does not end there. There is the funeral where 1,000 people paid their respects and tell you how wonderful your son is and how he positively changed their lives.

You receive your son's death certificate. His name, Robert, is in black and white. Can you imagine reading that?

Daily you visit his grave and cry endless tears. Months pass, during which you grieve. You question your faith. Music hurts your ears. Nothing on television can distract you. Still you must clean out his personal belongings and sell his condo, his car, his beloved Harley. Have you stood by your child's grave viewing your newest purchase, the headstone with his name, Robert, so deeply etched?

Near my washing machine is the basket of clothes he brought home to launder. I cannot bear to wash them. There are endless telephone calls to lawyers, bank managers, college loan administrators, anywhere Robert had completed business transactions and where explanations have to be made that your son was killed by a drunken driver. So many people tell you they are sorry. You cry. There is no joy in my life, as I liken my life to living in hell. Life goes on, but I feel dead inside. My children were my world. Now one has been taken from me forever. Robert was needlessly murdered by a selfish drunken driver.

We filed House Bill #3768 and spoke before the Judiciary Committee in Boston to increase the penalty for Driving Under the Influence of Liquor and Drugs. We learned from the District Attorney that the penalty for Vehicular Homicide While Driving Under the Influence is not the same as other methods of killing a human being. What has impacted me the most during this time has been reading the newspaper each day. The reality of reading about the sentences other criminals receive for their crimes, all while their victims are still alive, is almost overwhelming. Here are some examples:

- In Springfield, X was sentenced to 7-10 years for trafficking cocaine. In the same case, XX was sentenced to nine to ten years.
- X of Springfield, was found guilty of mayhem and was sentenced to three to four years in State prison for biting off part of the ear of a coach at a youth basketball game.
- X of West Springfield, was sentenced for wire fraud, embezzlement from pension funds and money laundering. He received five years in prison.
- X received a sentence of thirty years for luring girls into sexual relationships over the internet.

I do not mean to imply these sentences were not fair and just, or the victims did not suffer from the injustices that were perpetrated on them. They are still alive. Robert is dead. He has no future.

X was sentenced to a mandatory life sentence for gunning down an innocent victim, 16 year old Brittany, in her own home. How is her death any different from my Robert's death? He also was an innocent victim of murder.

My question for you, Judge, is this: Why is vehicular homicide, driving under the influence, looked at differently than any other homicide? An article written in *The Republican*, in March, stated that twenty-seven homicides occurred in the Pioneer Valley in 2011. I wrote to him and asked why Robert's name was left off the list. He too was a homicide victim. I received no response.

When a person is killed by a gun or knife, it is not called a gun homicide or a knife homicide. A vehicle does not have the ability to drive itself any more than a gun or knife can maneuver itself. But, society almost views vehicular homicide as the vehicle being the object that did the killing. When, in fact, the person driving that vehicle caused the death the same as the person with a gun or knife caused a death. All are homicides. The defendant knowingly drank enough to be at double the legal limit for driving intoxicated, sat behind the wheel, knocked down two mailboxes, and drove into my son Robert as he stood in a driveway.

I am asking the court to please consider the death of my son and the killing of any other people by drunken drivers for what it is: murder. People who drink excessively, and then drive a two thousand pound vehicle, and plow into innocent people understand the ramifications of their actions. They are personally responsible for a murder. They just hope they won't get caught driving while intoxicated. But, Robert was murdered and knowing that the defendant faces such a short punishment just adds to my grief and despair. Massachusetts law gives you, Judge, the discretion to give a punishment for up to fifteen years. I plead with you to send the message to drunk drivers that they are accountable for their actions. This was not an accident. This was a choice made by a driver who chose to drive drunk. Every act has a consequence. Please sentence the defendant to the maximum allowed by Massachusetts law: fifteen years in a state penitentiary. Do not allow him to ever drive again. Make him tell other people who are convicted of drunk driving how his actions took the life of my son. Let his life have an impact on preventing another senseless death.

What would be justice for your child? Thirty days? Two and a half years? Fifteen years, or life?

I have a life sentence without Robert.

I plead for that same justice for my son, Robert.

During the year of the trial Mary Anne and her husband bought a small cottage on the Maine coast in order to live closer to their daughter. They have named the cottage Robert's Place, a serene spot where they have constant reminders of their son, as his furniture, dishes, pots, and pictures now live here instead of in their basement at home. Mary Anne decided to paint sunflowers on the kitchen wall to make it cheery and bright. She selected sunflowers because Steven and Robert used to compete to see who could grow the tallest sunflowers.

Two months after buying the cottage, Mary Anne was walking down a beach sand path and on the side in the tall sea grass she found a twelve inch sunflower plant with a single flower. The following week she saw it had been pulled up by its roots; she picked it up and planted it in their cottage yard. Also on this beach, a week before the trial, Mary Anne saw an inverted rainbow that looked like a smile. It is called a circumzenithal arc, and has been referred to as "a smile in the sky." To Mary Anne these are all signs from Robert, saying to her, "All will be well, Mom." She listens, and she begins to heal.

Resources:
www.MADD.org
www.compassionatefriends.org

Drunk Driving Statistics:
- The average drunk driver has driven drunk eighty times before first arrest.
- Every day in America, another twenty-eight people die as a result of drunk driving crashes.
- Every fifty-one minutes someone is killed in a drunk driving crash. Every ninety seconds someone is injured.
- Fifty to seventy-five percent of drunk drivers continue to drive on a suspended license.
- About one third of drunk driving problems—arrests, crashes, death, and injuries—come from repeat offenders.
- In 2013, 10,322 people died in drunk driving crashes—one every fifty-one minutes—and 290,000 were injured in drunk driving crashes.
- Each day people drive drunk almost 300,000 times in the US, but fewer than 4,000 are arrested.
- Drunk driving costs the US $199 billion a year.
- Campaign to Eliminate Drunk Driving launched by MADD in 2006.

Chapter 18
Marital Loyalty: Two Peas in a Pod
Helene

I MET CAROL and Don over 20 years ago when I was prescribing her anti-anxiety medications at a psychiatric out-patient clinic. Carol's anxiety disorder had been so severe she developed agoraphobia and hadn't left home for several years. Agoraphobia develops in reaction to panic attacks that are so terrifying the person will do almost anything to avoid having one, including totally isolating herself. During her young adulthood, Carol drank a good deal of alcohol to deal with her anxiety. By the time we met, Carol was no longer drinking, but depended on high doses of tranquillizers to get through each day and leave the house.

Throughout each ordeal, Carol's husband Don stayed by her side. Once she was able to go out of the house, they did everything together. Carol was prescribed Xanax when it was a new medication and physicians were not so afraid of causing addiction. When I took over her care, she informed me that large doses were necessary to give her the courage to leave home. She also still required company when she ventured out. She and Don talked delightedly about their grown children and grandchildren. She had been able to manage her anxiety enough to fly cross country for a family holiday visit. Don was approaching retirement and they looked forward to more trips together and increased time with the grandkids.

The first time I met them (I say *them* because until Don died, he attended all her appointments) they were wearing matching bowling jackets. They always sat close together, like two peas in a pod, often finishing each other's sentences. No matter how difficult the situation, there was always a great deal of laughter.

Sadly, a few years into treatment, Carol learned her liver was damaged from her previous alcohol use. As her health continued to fail, she lost an enormous amount of weight and was close to being on a transplant list. She began to show jaundice, a yellowing of the skin from toxins accumulating in the blood because of liver failure. Miraculously, under excellent medical care, Carol's health began to improve, foreshadowing her need to take over the supportive role Don had provided for her over the years.

One day, shortly after Don's retirement, Carol and Don came to her appointment with concern about a tiny lesion under Don's nail. The area was being biopsied by their physician. When I looked at his hand, I saw what appeared to be a thin sliver under one fingernail, surrounded by some inflammation. We all hoped for the best, but the insignificant lesion turned out to be melanoma of a most aggressive variety. Carol and Don dealt with this news and the treatments that followed as bravely as they dealt with her liver disease. Chemotherapy could not halt the disease, which metastasized rapidly. Within a year, Don was dead.

I grieved the loss of Don and also felt frightened for Carol. I worried that she might become suicidal (although that had never been a concern before) or start drinking again. I wondered how she could survive without her beloved life partner. But during a telephone check-in with me she sounded surprisingly well.

Carol told me that during Don's last days, he was in a great deal of pain. She stayed at his bedside in the hospital as he grew weaker and fought to stay alive. Carol realized he didn't want to leave her alone. "I told him I'd be okay; we'd be together again in the future; I told him he could go."

I knew Carol's heart must've broken when she gave that message to Don, and her voice quavered as she recalled the moment. She and I knew the significance of those words for her and the amount of courage and faith it took for her to say them.

Carol taught me how true love can create great generosity of spirit and willingness to do what is best for a loved one, even if that means letting go and being alone. Sometime later, Carol spoke of her enduring love for and closeness to Don. She said she could often feel his presence during the day and she talked to him every night. She felt content knowing she gave him a great gift in his time of need, just as he supported her all those years. Her voice still reflects her deep love for Don.

Chapter Nineteen
Death of a Spouse: My Forever Dance Partner
Patricia

DELORES ENTERED MY office at the urging of her five grown children. They were concerned about their mother and worried she wasn't getting over the death of their father. He had died over a year earlier and they thought their mother should be further along in grieving and getting back to her regular activities of life.

When Delores walked into my office I immediately noticed she had a spring to her step and a ready, beautiful smile. She is one of those lovely seventy-something women with milky skin and twinkly eyes, who greets you with, "Hello, dear, it's so nice to meet you." I immediately felt loved and welcomed by her, even though she was the one entering my office.

She wore a simple blouse and skirt and had her graying hair at just below her ear lobe, with a natural curl keeping it from her face. I told myself, "What a lovely woman; so natural and kind." She began by telling me she came to see me because she loved her five children and would do anything for them, even though she didn't think counseling was necessary. She related that her husband had died over a year earlier, after she had cared for him for several years. He had a condition called Lewy body dementia, something I hadn't heard of at the time, but soon researched in order to get a better understanding of what Delores was up against. She told me the dying process was terrible, with her husband Jake hallucinating and having outbursts—just not being himself. She said she was glad she had the years to care for him and is just now, fifteen months later, realizing he is gone.

When I asked about her marriage she spoke with such glowing terms that I could only think of Nicholas Sparks' novel, *The Notebook,* as she told me her love story. She and Jake were eighteen and nineteen when they eloped, so much in love they couldn't wait for a formal wedding. In those days, if you were "making love," then you married, she simply stated. Delores said, "Neither set of parents was pleased by our elopement and we started our married life very much alone, without support or encouragement from either family."

Their first baby came nine months later, and gradually their families began to accept this marriage. Jake worked as a laborer and she was a mother and housewife. She loved every day of her fifty-four year marriage to her husband. She spoke of how they loved dancing and the many camping trips with their five children. She said her husband, Jake, was the most handsome man she had ever known. I told myself, "And I know you were the most beautiful woman he ever knew."

Delores and I became fast friends as I asked her to tell me more about her love story. Her eyes lit up whenever she spoke of Jake, except when she talked about his last years. Then her eyes expressed a deep sadness and loss. She told me her children were concerned about her because she didn't want to attend many social events, except family gatherings. And they were also worried that she spoke too much about her love for their Dad. The more we talked, the more convinced I felt that Delores was fine, and that she was simply grieving the love of her life. After a couple sessions, I told her that I thought she didn't need to see me and I felt she was having a normal grief. She seemed relieved. and then said maybe she should share something with me before she left, just to make sure I did not think she was crazy.

"Oh, no," I thought. "What could Delores have to share with me? Perhaps I suggested ending therapy too soon."

Shyly, she told me, almost like a confession, that every night, after she cleaned up her dinner dishes she turned on some old dancing records she and Jake listened to over the years. She would get out her favorite broom, lift it to Jake's six foot two height, and dance with "him" for fifteen to twenty minutes. She looked forward to this more than any other part of her day. Delores quizzically looked at me to see how I would respond.

I smiled at her with tears in my eyes and said, "How lovely."

She beamed and said, "You know, Dr. Martin, many people would say that was crazy, but I knew you'd understand. When you love someone the way I love Jake, your love never dies. You just have to remember that and you'll be able to dance with him forever. I know he isn't with me in my day-to-day life anymore, but he is with me for those special fifteen minutes every night."

As we parted, I gave her a hug goodbye, and thanked her for teaching me so much about eternal love.

Resources:

www.mayoclinic.org/diseases/Lewy Body Dementia definition:

1. Lewy body dementia, the second most common type of progressive dementia after Alzheimer's disease, causes a progressive decline in mental abilities. It may also cause hallucinations, which generally take the form of objects, people or animals that aren't there. This can lead to unusual behavior such as having conversations with deceased loved ones. Another indicator of Lewy body dementia may be significant fluctuations in alertness and attention, which may include daytime drowsiness or periods of staring into space. And, like Parkinson's disease, Lewy body dementia can result in rigid muscles, slowed movement, and tremors. In Lewy body dementia, protein deposits, called Lewy bodies, develop in nerve cells in regions of your brain involved in thinking, memory, and movement (motor control).

2. *The Notebook*, by Nicholas Sparks, Warner Books, 1996.

Words of wisdom from Delores: "Make love for as long as you are able!"

Poem from *She Walks in Beauty: A Woman's Journey Through Poems*, 2011, New York: Hyperion Press, compiled by Caroline Kennedy.

To My Dear and Loving Husband,

by Anne Broadstreet

If ever two were one, then surely we.
If ever man were lov'd by wife, then thee;
If ever wife was happy in a man,
Compare with me ye women if you can.
I prize thy love more than whole mines of gold,
Or all the riches that the East doth hold.
My love is such that rivers cannot quench,
Nor Aught but love from thee, give recompense.
Thy love is such I can no way repay,
The heavens reward thee manifold, I pray.
Then while we live, in love let's so persever
That, when we live no more, we may live ever.

Chapter 20
Mother Courage: Living On After a Death
Patricia

WE LEARN MANY lessons from our mothers during our lifetimes. And if we're fortunate to have a good mother, life lessons may include examples of kindness, resilience, generosity, friendliness, gratitude, open-mindedness, simplicity, and assertiveness. We might learn specific behaviors called *manners*, such as how to behave at the dinner table, greeting guests, and sending thank-you cards. We learn to say "please" and "thank you." We learn household tasks such as washing dishes, setting the table, sewing on a button, and making a bed. If we're lucky, we learn to cook.

A mother may teach you to solve problems with girlfriends or boyfriends. She may be the shoulder to cry on when you learn tough lessons. If you're part of a large family, you learn to share with siblings. You might have opportunities to develop your talents in sports, dance, music lessons, or art classes. A mother may take you on special outings, just the two of you. She may encourage you to further your education, even if she didn't have the same opportunities.

A mother may show you how to love and be a good friend. She might encourage you to show gratitude and perform acts of kindness. She may suggest you have fun every day in some way—laugh out loud, sing if you feel like it, dance! Just do it! Don't worry if your house is perfectly clean, or your food gourmet; just get friends together and have fun.

A mother may teach you how to be assertive and not let people take advantage of you. She may teach you to treat those who appear weak with tenderness and care. She may show you generosity of spirit in everyday life, but also demonstrate how to stand up for what you believe even when others oppose you. She may show you the power of prayer and how to handle adversity or illness by taking a positive "we can beat this" attitude.

You may learn the love of travel from your mother—to going on adventures to see the world, even if the world is only your town. She may teach you, in the face of natural beauty, to close your eyes and take a snapshot in your mind. Then you can cherish each memory forever.

I am fortunate to have a mother who taught me all of these things. My mother contributed to my personhood in many ways and also helped me raise my own children. And now, at the age of eighty-six, my mother is still teaching me—and this may be the greatest lesson of all: how to have courage and continue on after the loss of my father, her husband of sixty-two years.

At the wake and funeral in September she said she had to be strong because she knew my father's death was hard on each of his five children, fourteen grandchildren, and six great-grandchildren. She could see the granddaughters were especially broken up, so she tried her best not to fall apart while we were all together.

Another example of Mom's bravery was in November when she took her first trip alone via airplane to visit me, because my father was being honored at a Veteran's Day event in our local town. With wheelchair assistance she managed to make a transfer in Charlotte and then flew on to Hartford. During her visit I hosted a gathering of friends to celebrate Mom, and she was given a crown and read a lovely tribute poem written by a friend.

In spite of her brave face, I know my mother goes through many lonely days. She told me she doesn't understand why God has it all wrong in making people of long marriages die separately. She thinks God should let them die together. She laughs and says, "I'm so bossy, telling God how to do things."

I say, "God has it right. It would be devastating for us children if we lost both of you at the same time."

She and I cry together often when we share memories of Dad or share dreams we now have that include my father. She says it's so hard to lose him because he was such a good man. I know mornings are toughest for her, when they would have their morning tea and coffee and my dad would tell his Dolores how beautiful she is and give her a hug. Now she watches Mass on TV to fill the morning hours. She has lady friends in her community who are also widows and they go to lunch, movies, and the theater. She heads a Caring Committee that sends cards and meals to people in her town.

My mother showed courage most recently by deciding to host a New Year's Eve party at her home. She called the thirty home owners in her 55+ community and individually asked them to her house for a New Year's Eve party by singing a song "What are you doing New Year's Eve?"—a tune sung by Rosemary Clooney.

She says every person agreed to come and her house was filled with over thirty guests. The average age was eighty-two. The arrival time was 6:30 p.m., with Mom having those in wheelchairs arrive a bit earlier to get settled. They drank mimosas and poinsettias to toast the New Year (orange juice and champagne, and cranberry juice and champagne). At one point she walked around her house and noticed groups of men sitting and talking in one room, while the women were chatting around a table in another part of the house. She felt delighted to have planned a wonderful event for people who would normally spend New Year's Eve alone. She was glad to bring joy into their lives. For some, it might have been their last New Year's Eve.

Around 9:30 p.m. her guests began returning to their respective homes and her house was empty by ten o'clock. Mom asked her children not to call until New Year's Day so she wouldn't have to leave her party guests. I know she had a good cry when everyone left that evening, but it is so typical of Mom's courage and kindness to host a party for others and keep busy so as not to miss my Dad quite so much.

She has taught me from her actions that even the most difficult situations can be handled with grace and kindness. She gives herself time to grieve, yet continues on day by day, living her life without Dad. She tries to stay busy, connect with others, continue her daily rituals, and find purpose in her life. She is my Mother Courage.

This chapter taken in part from article, *Mother Imparts Lesson of Courage,* published in Mass-Live, May 1, 2014.

Chapter 21
Retirement: Breaking Up is Hard to Do

Helene

NOT TOO LONG AGO I had the experience of closing my small private practice and saying goodbye to clients, some of whom I'd treated for ten to twenty years. I couldn't help but compare the experience to having my children grow up and leave home.

I carefully chose the person who would continue with each of these clients, similar to the way I guided my daughters to the best college match for each of them. I made sure every new provider had the information necessary for a seamless transfer.

So why did I experience two weeks of worry and dream-filled nights?

At the end of two weeks I was attending a favorite yoga class and struggled to empty my mind of chatter so I could benefit from deep relaxation. I found myself caught up in these familiar worries about leaving my practice when an inner voice came to me saying, "Just as with your children, you've given your clients the tools to deal with life, both the good and the bad. They are prepared to leave and take the next step."

I immediately relaxed, entered into relaxation, and no longer experienced the recurrent dreams.

Retirement, whether full or partial, is an emotional time filled with new challenges and experiences—and also filled with endings. So many of life's transitions contain mixed feelings of regret and anticipation. The better prepared we are, the smoother the passage.

Chapter 22
The Final Goodbye: A Death of a Patient
Helene

LETTING GO OF someone we love is a form of saying goodbye that rings with finality.

Kissing an adult child as she departs from a weekend visit back to her separate life can be emotionally wrenching.

Holding a cherished pet as his life is extinguished is heart breaking.

Being with a parent who draws the last breath is difficult, but it can be a gift.

Shortly before I had to deal with the deaths of my own parents, one of my clients, Ruth, said a final good-bye to both her parents as they lay terminally ill in their hospital beds. Both had lived long lives. Ruth experienced unspeakable trauma from them as a child, but she put that aside to nurse them, comfort them, show compassion, forgive them, and finally let them go. She was present when both parents took their last breaths and she took comfort in knowing she did everything she could to ease their transition. In doing all that, she freed herself.

Living vicariously through Ruth's experience helped prepare me for my own impending bereavement. Any resentment I felt seemed miniscule in comparison to her experience and her ability to forgive. My mother experienced an agonizingly slow death from congestive heart failure at age 86. I felt frustration and anger as I watched her suffer for weeks. The heart that was killing her refused to stop beating. This was one of the most helpless feelings I've ever had. Seven years later my father died at age 95 from stage IV liver cancer, undiagnosed until three weeks before his death. His passing seemed more peaceful to me. Both ended in hospice care in a warm, caring facility.

I thought of Ruth many times as I stayed by my parents' bedsides, and I recognized what a gift she bestowed on me by sharing her experience. I also recognized how fortunate I was to be there both times for my parents. The comfort I provided was rewarded by love returned and a good ending.

As a therapist, experiencing the death of a client is also heartbreaking. I watched a previously vivacious and attractive client suffer the ravages of an unfair and relentless disease that was emotionally wrenching to all the people in her life, including me. Elizabeth was an artist with awesome talent with whom I was privileged to work. She was a beautiful, Rubenesque woman with fair skin, full dark hair, and dark brown eyes that could shoot anger or sparkle with mirth. In our first meeting, she announced, "If this depression isn't better by 2000, I *will* be killing myself."

Thankfully, (and to Prozac's credit), she did improve, and about ten years later was as happy as I'd ever seen her. She and her long-time love were planning their wedding. I listened to her excited chatter about the specially ordered dress that would coordinate beautifully with her fiancé's dress kilt. Shortly after that happy announcement she was diagnosed with an especially deadly form of breast cancer. She struggled through the painful and debilitating treatments with her love at her side. Often she displayed her wry sense of humor as she pointed out her life-long battle with weight had resolved. She seemed to be half her size, as though she were slowly disappearing. She married before her death, but not in the way she had dreamed.

Every person we lose, whether it be a family member, friend, or client, leaves an ache in our hearts. But how our lives have been enriched by knowing them!

Having Children

Chapter 23
Dealing with Infertility and Disappointment: Waiting for Henry

Helene

WE HAD ADJUSTED as well as we could to a grandchildless life, filling our lives with work, friends, family, and exciting travel. The omnipresent question, "Any grandchildren?" would continue to sting, but only occasionally did a sense of sadness, of something missing, creep in. Generally it was an avoidant response, almost looking away when the countless pictures of adorable grandchildren were flashed in our faces; avoiding the handmade clothes and toys at craft fairs. Our sense of loss slammed into us in England, when good friends introduced us to their precocious and precious three year old son. After a wonderful afternoon visit, shortly before boarding the train back to London, little Raffie called me Nana. All I had been missing hit me at once, and I could see the sadness cross my husband's face as well.

After that encounter, I found myself praying hard to the Prague Infant Baby Jesus and a myriad of saints throughout Europe, as well as the Virgin Mother. I prayed not so much to change my daughters' minds, but that, if we were meant to be grandparents, these special people would facilitate it. Did I mention that I'm a Protestant, not Catholic?

Sometimes I felt anger building toward the young women I treated who thoughtlessly and easily had countless children. I felt even worse when hearing of serial abortions that were an extreme form of birth control following sexual carelessness.

A lovely patient of mine, herself a nurse and my daughter's age, gave kind encouragement after giving birth to twins after five IVF attempts.

Our younger daughter changed her mind about having children in her early thirties. Like many of her generation, years of pursuing a career and cultivating friendships gave way to yearning for a family. Sadly, a good portion of these young women encounter fertility problems. Our emotional roller coaster mirrored hers and her husband's: the joy at hearing her change of heart followed by the description of invasive fertility treatments, culminating in a successful IVF (in vitro fertilization). Each moment of relief would be followed by weeks of anxiety. I worked hard to restrain my calls and questions, knowing, or at least suspecting, what they were going through. I was unaware of the significance of "two weeks" until an embryo was transferred from the petri dish to our daughter's eager uterine lining. At two weeks a test determines if the woman is pregnant and the transfer was a success. This waiting is followed by countless tests and benchmarks and false scares. I tried hard not to get too emotionally invested in this new being, but seeing him as the "dancing baby bean" at two months won my heart. Each ultrasound brought more reassurances.

When our daughter was close to three months pregnant, I needed an MRI of my shoulder. It was a last minute decision the day of Superstorm Sandy, and I grabbed at the opportunity without fully thinking out the process. While I lay in the tube with its incessant pounding drowning out the "spa" music I had mistakenly chosen (next time it will be rap), I practiced my yoga breathing and visualized my little grandchild in my lap. The sense of holding him comforted me and brought me through the MRI with a smile on my face. The tech said with a perplexed look, "You really did well." Henry had become real to me at that moment. I visualized him for the next six months as I prayed to keep him safe from harm.

As my daughter's pregnancy drew to a close, the anxiety returned. Every phone call was an alarm. I packed my own "go bag" so I could leap on the train in a moment's notice. I arranged my work in Massachusetts so as to be with her and her family the month of April (the baby was due on April 7). My husband and I worried the baby would be late, causing us to waste precious time as we anxiously waited in our Brooklyn apartment. We were fortunate to have an apartment a few subway stops from our daughter.

Various symptoms of impending labor preceded a midnight call from our son-in-law. Our daughter had been admitted after her water broke at home. Later she told us she'd been creating Ecards for Easter at 9 p.m. and heard the sound of the water tearing away just as she pressed "send." Needless to say, we were awake much of the night. Fortunately we'd already arranged for a car to drive us to Brooklyn the Monday after Easter, so decisions about when to leave were settled.

I finally got out of bed at 6:15 a.m., knowing I wouldn't fall back asleep. The familiar anxiety returned as I started reviewing all the complications of prolonged labor. An hour later I hesitantly texted my son-in-law. I didn't want to intrude, but felt compelled to know.

"How are you all doing?"

"Why don't you see for yourself?" he responded and attached a picture of our beautiful daughter holding their son Henry, who entered the world at 6:15 a.m.

We joyously went to church and had the minister make our announcement. Good friends had been praying for Henry for months. A friend's eyes filled up with tears when I told her the news prior to the service: "He was born at sunrise" she said. Easter sunrise is special to Christians, as is Handel's "Alleluia Chorus" which my husband said was especially meaningful that day.

After church we walked around the side of the building to the Memorial Garden where both my parents' ashes are buried. My mother had a younger brother, Henry, who was special to her and died in his fifties. My parents had loved Easter and celebrated it with new outfits, Easter baskets, family portraits, and gourmet dinners ending with homemade bunny cakes, decorated with flowers. I chose Easter for my father's memorial service in 2007. On this special Easter, I could sense their joy as well.

Now that we've met Henry, we can't keep our eyes off him and are honored to be able to help in these early weeks. I recently told my daughter I had no idea how much her father wanted a grandchild until she became pregnant. It's one of the few times I've seen him cry. We were kidding ourselves that we made a good adjustment to being grandchildless.

Infertility Treatments

At age thirty-five, a woman's chance of getting pregnant decreases and the risk of miscarriage goes up. A thorough evaluation must be made of the male and female's health and fertility. Medications may be given to stimulate ovulation or treat polycystic ovarian syndrome. Blocked fallopian tubes which carry the eggs to the uterus may require surgery. Endometriosis (a painful, chronic gynecological disease) needs to be ruled out as well. If the male partner or donor's sperm count is low, the sperm may require concentration. It can then be placed in the woman's uterus at the time of ovulation (IUI—intrauterine insemination), to increase the chance of successful fertilization.

If none of these less invasive treatments are successful (but to the participants be assured they are highly invasive) in producing a pregnancy, IVF (in vitro fertilization) may be recommended. Insurance coverage is variable and the cost may be prohibitive. The treatment is time intensive and invasive, requiring many medical examinations, meticulous tracking of the menstrual cycle, and hormonal medications that culminate in two weeks of self-administered injections. Following the injections, the woman's eggs are retrieved at the right moment of her cycle, after which they are fertilized with the partner's or donor's sperm. Viable embryos are transferred to the uterine lining shortly after. Success rates vary with the institutions performing the procedures, the mother's age, and many other factors. Needless to say this whole process requires tremendous commitment from the participants and many days away from work and other activities. Watchful waiting is necessary at all steps. The entire process creates anxiety for prospective parents, but when successful, it also brings great joy.

Chapter 24
The Donor Egg: Trying is Trying
Patricia

DURING A LIFETIME, we each face many choices that have a profound impact on our lives. I believe the most important decision, with the greatest lifelong impact, is whether or not to have children. Many of us don't stop to think about having kids, because we assume it's part of being married. We may even find ourselves unintentionally pregnant, but no matter how or when we become parents, we take on a lifetime commitment. I think of it as a responsibility and concern that stretches from womb to tomb or from cradle to grave. Parenting is truly a lifelong journey when we choose to keep and raise our children.

For some of us, including myself, getting pregnant was easy. No problems with fertility in my life—just say the word and we were pregnant. Lucky us! My husband would say he just had to walk past the bedroom door and I would conceive. But I realize many other people have a difficult time becoming parents. Such was the case with Lisa and Kevin, a couple who desperately wanted children, yet found it impossible to sustain a pregnancy. My role as a psychologist in this process was to help them explore conception options and then offer compassion and kindness during their many losses over years of trying. When Lisa first came to see me, she was desperate to become a mother and forlorn over several miscarriages and futile attempts to conceive. I will never forget her first words: "Dr. Martin, trying is so trying."

As she relayed her history up to that time, I realized how difficult the journey had been, yet she still wasn't ready to give up hope. Lisa was thirty-nine years old when she began counseling with me, and she'd already spent seven years trying to conceive a child. Although I could tell she was tired and depressed about the failures, she used humor to lighten her frustration. Her wit was dry and dark at times, yet it helped her cope through this challenging process. Underneath the exterior of jocularity hid a frustrated, anxious, depressed woman desperate to become a mother. After a few sessions I concluded I could best help Lisa by listening to her stories of loss and helping her seek new options.

Lisa was a thirty-two year old, married, college educated woman when she and her engineer husband, Kevin, decided to have children. She worked as a freelance photographer and had started her own photography business. Since her grandmother had nine children, Lisa assumed conceiving a child would be a breeze. After a year of trying without a pregnancy, she visited a specialist who prescribed Clomid, a drug that increases fertility. As Lisa said, "Before long I was getting coolers full of hormonal cocktails and injecting myself in public bathrooms and cars." She went on to say, "There was nothing pleasant about the process whatsoever; it was invasive, degrading, and sad. In hindsight, Clomid was my gateway drug."

Lisa and her husband experienced five failed intrauterine inseminations (IUIs). She told me, "Each failed attempt was lengthy, complicated, and more devastating than the last. Each one took away a little piece of me." She and Kevin, who put faith in the scientific process, started trying Chinese herbs and acupuncture. She had countless good luck charms and Kevin had his lucky boxer shorts.

The final IUI when Lisa was thirty-five years old resulted in a pregnancy with triplets. She was elated, yet terrified. She joked, "There's a reason Hallmark card stores have a twin section, because of all the fertility methods."

Sadly, after about eight weeks, one of the heartbeats stopped and the next ultrasound showed the other two hearts had slowed. Lisa was told to wait through the weekend and come back on Monday. She describes this as "one of the most painful weekends I ever endured. I vividly imagined the horror of the death that was occurring within my body. I had nightmares. We had waited so long, we tried so hard. It didn't matter."

On Monday the doctor confirmed the final two heartbeats had stopped. Lisa had the removal procedure and awakened from the anesthesia hysterically sobbing that she had lost her babies. She remembers kind nurses and warm blankets. During the next week, while wandering around in a haze, Lisa purchased three rocks with HOPE chiseled in them. She cried at the checkout counter.

The doctors decided it was time to up the ante. They increased the drugs and Lisa and Kevin progressed to in vitro fertilization (IVF). They tried 4 IVF cycles that failed, each time becoming increasingly taxing. Somewhere in her chart Lisa read her condition listed as "decreased ovarian reserve." She did not have the expected quantity and quality of eggs for someone her age. No one knew why. She remembers battles with insurance companies to get the cycles covered. During this time period Lisa sought counseling for depression.

After the fourth IVF failed, the doctor recommended looking into donor eggs or adoption. Lisa felt devastated, as though her support team had given up on her. She and Kevin sought a second opinion and the recommendation was a donor egg. However, she decided to try one more IVF cycle with a new team. She had renewed hope, a new team, a big name hospital, and a renowned expert. Her humor kicked in again when she passed a sign outside the hospital, Safe Baby Drop Off. This was where mothers could drop off babies they couldn't care for and the hospital would take care of them until they could be placed in foster care. Lisa joked that she and her husband should just stand in front of the sign with their arms open.

Yet another "big box of drugs" arrived. She had her regular cry while opening them, angry that she couldn't just have sex to get a baby like everyone else. "This felt so unnatural, so aggressive, so not *me*."

The physicians were only able to extract two eggs, of which only one embryo survived. They placed this last hope embryo in her uterus—and surprisingly Lisa became pregnant. THIS time would be it, she thought. They drove for the ultrasound two months later to see the little baby growing.

"We could tell by the look on the technician's face that it was bad news for us yet again." Lisa miscarried two weeks later, then had another D&C procedure. She asked for a part of the tissue to bring home to bury. "I hated going into the hospital pregnant and leaving with nothing. My obstetrician obliged and we planted a Japanese maple on the burial site. Looking at it today still makes my stomach ache."

While Kevin was in the waiting area of the hospital he found a brochure from an infertility support group called Resolve. They were having an informational seminar for people considering donor egg or adoption. Even though emotionally raw, just a week after her miscarriage, Lisa and Kevin attended the meeting to just go and listen. At this meeting Lisa learned she and Kevin had been in this battle years longer than anyone in the room.

Lisa said, "The most useful portion of the seminar was when couples spoke who had adopted or used a donor egg to create their family. I remember asking through tears what it felt like to not be able to pass on your genetics and how could you ever recover from that loss. I was sure I never would. Couple after couple assured me that once you have your child, that loss becomes less important. I didn't believe them and was sure they had to convince themselves of that because they had no other choice."

The experience at the Resolve meeting changed Lisa's outlook; she and Kevin decided to try a donor egg. After careful consideration, Lisa sent a letter to a relative in her early twenties who worked in a medical field. Lisa thought this woman would be a great donor. She declined. They then went through the search with their fertility doctors, reviewing for potential donors. Lisa described the process as surreal: "They asked us questions like did we care how the donor looked; was extended family medical history relevant, and how far back would it be relevant?" Lisa joked it was similar to trying to date online, but with greater consequences.

A few weeks later, while hosting a photography exhibit, Lisa was approached by one of her second cousins, Molly, who offered to learn more about potentially donating eggs. Lisa remembers the room spinning as she received this generous offer. Lisa and Kevin met with Molly the next week and shared all the concerns she should consider, giving her every opportunity to back out. She still said, "Yes!" The very same day the hospital called and said they had matched a donor to Lisa and Kevin's criteria. Two potential donors in one week—maybe their luck was changing. Lisa quickly realized she preferred having a relative as the donor, so she would have genes in common with their child from one side of her family. Molly was a bright, thoughtful woman who clearly understood the ramifications of egg donation. Lisa took comfort in that.

She said, "Still, it was strange, and I felt like a failure because I needed help from another woman to conceive. They'd be using Molly's egg and my husband's sperm. Sometimes that made me cringe a little, but I felt we could work through it. We'd already been through so much. The challenges of being at the forefront of fertility science seemed miniscule and even exciting compared to a life where I could never be pregnant and give birth to our baby."

She continues, "At the same time, I occasionally mourned for the loss of my imagined children who would look like me and carry half my genes. But I had faith that I could step into this new idea of family."

The legal paperwork was completed. Thinking about what her cousin went through for her still brings tears to Lisa's eyes. This generous gift renewed Lisa's belief that no matter what situation she is in, someone will always rise to the occasion and lend a selfless hand.

The eggs were retrieved from the donor, a whopping sixteen eggs. Lisa was shocked as her own retrievals on much more aggressive protocols were in the low single digits. She and Kevin once again joked it was time to buy a tour van. After five days, only two eggs survived. The team chose the best embryo and placed it into Lisa's uterus. She sobbed when the procedure was complete, as she had done every time before. Technically, she was pregnant, she always thought. Now began the two week wait to see if the blood test confirmed pregnancy. It did; and nine months later a beautiful little girl was born, who received Lisa's family surname as her first name.

Three years later at forty-two years of age, Lisa decided to try pregnancy again with the second retrieved embryo. Given things had gone so perfectly the first time, Lisa was sure it would work. It did not. Again, Lisa was devastated. Their cousin donor, Molly had since married and was about to start her own family, so she was in no position to donate. While the pain was different for Lisa because she had a daughter, it was still sadness and loss as she longed for a sibling for her child.

Not being one to give up, Lisa asked a first cousin, Bridget, on the other side of her family if she would consider donation. It seemed like a nice balance for Lisa to have a child from either side of her family. Since the first transferred embryo with their other donor resulted in a viable pregnancy, they assumed the same would happen with their second donor. Lisa says, "Again, all logic in our lives seemed to go out the window when we were involved in this emotional game."

The first transfer didn't work. Devastation again and all previous disappointments resurfaced. But they would try again. They waited another few months and tried a second embryo. Success! The pregnancy results were positive and they were done. They had a bonfire to burn the mountains of paperwork and another baby girl was born.

In total Kevin and Lisa spent ten years on the fertility process, trying to get pregnant, trying to maintain their sanity, and fending off the isolation and depression that come with endless disappointments. Lisa says, "It took a village to get me pregnant."

Most days Lisa is too busy to think about all she went through to bring her wonderful daughters into the world and the incredible effort from so many people that made it happen. Now Lisa has a strong need to lend an ear to others who are in the sad club of infertility. She started a support group and has formed caring friendships with several women, most whom have become pregnant as well. Lisa believes having someone to sit with in your pain is the best gift we have to give. She is forever appreciative to those who did so for her. I am forever grateful to Lisa for sharing her story.

Resources:

www.Resolve.org
www.fertilityauthority.com
www.fertilityguide.com
www.nationaladoptionday.org
www.fertilethoughts.com

Chapter 25

Coping with a Child's Cancer Diagnosis: Stay Positive

Patricia

MY WORK WITH families inevitably leads to having the mother of an ill child call me for counsel and guidance. As the mother of four grown children, I still shudder at the thought of serious illness befalling my loved ones. Therefore, when I begin working with a mother who has a chronically ill child I experience a multitude of emotions myself, including—

- sympathy and fear,
- trying to understand the clinical and scientific issues,
- offering comfort and support,
- and the ultimate feeling of awe and inspiration at the courage of these mothers.

One such mother was Leslie, a tall, lean, blond woman who always seemed tanned. She had a loud, ready laugh and a throaty voice that exposed years of cigarette smoking. Leslie is extraordinarily funny and fantastically brave. She came to see me after her son had been through five years of chemotherapy for leukemia. She needed help accepting that her marriage had failed and learning to move on and disengage from a controlling, abusive man. Leslie handled the years of caring for her son with grace and aplomb, but separating emotionally from the codependent relationship with her ex-husband felt like a huge burden.

When Leslie joined a support group I moderate for women in abusive relationships, she was an immediate hit with all the group members because of her wit. But under the disguise of joviality was a frightened woman with a lower than low self-esteem. Part of her recovery meant going back to school to earn an MBA that would help her run the non-profit corporation she started after her son was diagnosed. The corporation raises money through fundraisers to provide play materials to children who are in the hospital undergoing chemotherapy treatment. During group meetings Leslie would share some of her class assignments, which brought many of us to tears, and left us with a lasting impression of this gutsy woman.

Leslie quoted Nicholas Murray Butler in one of her essays: "Optimism is the foundation of courage." That six word statement summarizes Leslie. She writes:

What does Mom do when her healthy child is diagnosed with cancer?

What does Mom say when her child, as well as his siblings, look to her for the familiar words of reassurance? How does Mom hide her own fears, pain and helplessness to find any words, any confidence, any positive thing to say? How does Mom initially process her own feelings in order to be the nurturing person she needs to be for all her children?

In an instant, all Mom's tried and true magic healing tools are made irrelevant. How does she look into the eyes of her child and promote reassurances she knows could be a potential lie?

Leslie goes on to say that each mom needs to remind herself every day that this is about her child and how he feels, not herself. She knows that to be productive, each mother needs to bury those feelings of "why us" in the same vault where she hides her worst fears and feelings. She is steadfast in her desire to make this new journey as painless and trauma free as possible. She focuses solely on her child's needs and attempts to bring a sense to her child and herself that all is well. She is by his side every day, for every treatment, for every prolonged hospital stay, with a smile and a game, or conversation that hopefully involves laughter. She is there when he is struggling, both emotionally and physically. She is there when he overcomes challenges. She laughs and cries with him, and is humbled with respect for how brave this young person is, and how he endures the entire process. She acknowledges how difficult this is for him, and lets him do the same. She tells him how much she admires his courage and determination, especially on the bad days.

Leslie speaks to me and our group about how she does not feel brave or strong; she actually feels weak and fearful. But we all know this is a woman who took on the challenge of a sick child and succeeded in helping him be cancer free and remain a whole person in so many ways. She is a model for all of us; the selfless Mom who's able to smile and bring laughter to her son and other children throughout the extremes of cancer treatment. Here is a courageous mom. Here is Leslie, a valiant woman as described by Ernest Hemingway when he said, "Courage is grace under pressure."

As a postscript Leslie wanted me to share the words of her fourteen year old son who faced cancer and survived. She is proud of her son and believes her positive approach took seed in his heart.

Having cancer is like coming to a fork in the road, where both sides are initially bad. One side however, ends with more sorrow and defeat, and the other side ends with feeling accomplished and ready for whatever lies ahead in life. A common misconception many people have about cancer patients is that negativity cannot be taken out of the circumstances. They are blind to the fact that cancer patients, just like everyone else, have a choice. I made my choice early on. I decided I would remain positive and try to make the best out of everything, even if there was realistically nothing to be optimistic about. Realizing I did in fact have a choice to stay positive, made the whole process a little easier.

Resources:

www.cancercare.org
https://acco.org —Support online for parents
www.childrenscause.org

Chapter 26
A Mother Responds to Her Child's Sexual Abuse
Patricia and Helene

PARENTS HAVE DOZENS of problems to worry about on any given day: illness, accidents, grades, bullying, and a dozen other things life throws our way. It's always something. But few of us are prepared for the horrifying disclosure that a child has been sexually abused. When that abuse comes from a family member, the horror is magnified.

Considering the prevalence of child sexual abuse, it's no surprise that we've encountered many patients who were abused themselves or have a history of abuse in their families. The Centers for Disease Control and Prevention reports that one in four girls and one in six boys is a victim of child sexual abuse.[15] Sadly, a history of childhood sexual abuse may lead to a life of continued abuse and/or severe mental illness.

The intense feelings evoked by discovering your child has been sexually abused are complex and may include shock, rage, confusion, denial, disbelief, and guilt. Knowing your life and relationships with family, extended family, friends, and associates will be forever changed may cause intense and paralyzing fear. Relationships will be severed, loyalties will be divided. The emotional conflict is especially horrible when the alleged abuser is a loved person. If you depend on the alleged perpetrator for financial or emotional support the fear will be even worse. You may be torn between doing the right thing by addressing the abuse on the one hand, and protecting yourself and preventing things from changing on the

15 Center for Disease Control and Prevention (2005) *Adverse Childhood Experiences Study: Data and Statistics.* Atlanta, GA. National Center for Injury Prevention and Control. http://www.cdc.gov/nccdphp/ace/prevalence.htm

other hand. The rage in someone who has vowed to protect their children because of her own history of abuse can become murderous and dangerous.

So how is a parent supposed to behave following such a shocking disclosure? Experts agree that parental response plays a powerful role in how a child begins healing from the abuse. One of the most troublesome reactions from the mother is a sense of betrayal, not just by the abuser, but from her child who she may see as "the other woman" and the destroyer of the life she knows. If a parent goes into denial or refuses to listen to the child's report, the child will feel dismissed, abandoned, and betrayed by yet another family member. Many patients have told us that when they worked up the courage to tell their mothers they were being "touched" by a father, step-father, brother, uncle or grandfather, the mothers responded with anger and disgust at them and said, "I never want to hear you speak of this again. How dare you suggest that would happen!"

This refusal to believe causes abuse victims to shrink further into themselves and sink into shame and terror. If an adult they are supposed to trust doesn't believe them, then where can they turn? This is a tremendous burden for any child to carry, often resulting in serious mental health problems, physical health issues, or suicide.

On occasion, a mother has the courage and conviction to do the right thing. She may herself have been a victim of abuse and vows she will handle things differently if anything ever happens to her children. Such is the story of Joanna, a woman sexually abused by her stepfather, who was able to do the right thing when she learned her son was being molested.

Joanna had seen me in the past to work on her own anxiety issues. As our therapy progressed it became apparent her anxiety was biologically based, and also a reaction to childhood issues of abuse and not feeling in control of her life. As we explored her past abuse Joanna began to feel more and more in charge of her life. She became happier and able to live in a more spontaneous manner with less anxiety and worry.

She asked me to see her ten year old son who was having symptoms of anxiety, taking the form of obsessive and compulsive behaviors. He had a nightly ritual of checking that all his toys were lined up properly, or he would have to go to the bathroom three times before going to bed. When he began washing his hands to the point of developing chafing and eczema, Joanna was worried and asked me to see him. Upon meeting Tommy, I could tell he was anxious, but he attributed his "nervousness" to worrying about school. He was anxious about the standardized state tests and wanted to get good grades. For him, good grades meant ninety percent and above because he wanted all A's.

In this competitive world I often see children with anxiety, much of it due to school stress and peer pressure. I knew some of his obsessive and compulsive behaviors might be caused by academic stress. I inquired if he had other stressors at home and as part of my routine screening, I asked, "Has anyone ever touched your private parts in a way that made you feel uncomfortable?"

He looked at me quizzically and vehemently said, "No, yuck!"

I let it go at that point. We worked on some cognitive behavioral strategies to help with his anxiety. I taught him ways to relax on a daily basis, and we spoke about how he often catastrophized situations and made them much worse than they actually were. He took well to "cognitive restructuring," which helped reduce his anxiety symptoms. He was able to talk to himself in a healthy fashion when he started to feel stressed by saying things like, "It's okay if I don't get an "A" on this test; I'll just give it a good try by studying and preparing, and whatever the result will be okay."

Or before going to bed, he would listen to a relaxation app on his iPhone and tell himself he only needed to go to the bathroom once. When he got into bed he would put on his relaxation app and fall asleep. I continued to see Tommy on a monthly basis just to keep him on track and monitor his anxiety. All seemed to be going well.

About a year after I had started therapy with Tommy, Joanna called in a panic, saying her great aunt had called and was worried that Tommy had an "unhealthy" relationship with his paternal uncle. The great aunt, who had been sexually abused as a child, thought the uncle was a little too friendly with Tommy. Joanna asked me to talk to Tommy and see if this concern had any foundation. She said her great aunt sometimes tried to stir up trouble between the families and Joanna didn't want to get carried away by making accusations. Yet, she didn't want to ignore the accusation if it was true. I agreed to meet with Tommy and explore this concern.

Tommy and I started our session talking about everyday events at school with friends and discussing his favorite sports team. He loves the Red Sox, and I, too, follow them, so we often discussed the latest game. Finding common ground, like a sports team or musical group, helps establish a trusting alliance with an adult therapist for children and adolescents. I then began to talk about "good touch, bad touch" and asked if anyone had ever touched his private parts in a way that wasn't appropriate. He looked at me quizzically. I mentioned that sometimes even people we trust who are part of our families might do this, such as cousins, uncles, or grandparents. He said "No, no one in my family would do that."

There was a long pause and I could see he was thinking of something. I asked, "Has someone other than a family member touched your private area?"

Tommy looked at me innocently and said, "Well, there was a guy who worked at the bowling alley who would ask me to let him touch me. He would take me over to the side of the building and say I was very special and then he would rub his hand over my pants, down below."

I asked him to show me where the guy touched him. I then asked if this was still happening and how old he was when it first began. Tommy said it wasn't happening anymore because he didn't go to the bowling alley as an after school activity this year. It happened last year when he was in the sixth grade and occurred about six times.

I told him he had done nothing wrong, but I needed to tell his mom about this and he agreed it was okay. Even if he didn't want me to tell his mom, I would be required to disclose the information as a mandated reporter. I asked if he wanted to stay in the room when I spoke with his mom and he said he did. When Joanna came in, I told her Tommy had reported to me about someone touching him inappropriately. She was relieved to hear it wasn't her uncle, but dismayed to learn her son had been molested at a school sponsored after school activity.

Joanna kept her cool throughout our discussion. She asked me, "What should we do now?"

I suggested she contact the local police department and let them know this had happened because it was important to protect other children. After our session she immediately went to the bowling alley and learned the person who molested her son no longer worked there. She was able to get the man's first name from Tommy, so they could identify the perpetrator. Joanna and Tommy then went to their local police department and reported the incident.

The lieutenant investigating the case was kind and understanding toward Tommy and Joanna and told Tommy, "You didn't do anything wrong, and we're pleased you came to us so we can take care of this."

The police have apprehended the perpetrator, who is now a registered sex offender. He was found guilty and is awaiting sentencing. I followed up in therapy with Tommy about the sexual molestation and educated him about what is sexual abuse and what to do if someone tries to molest him. He listened attentively and nodded his head that he understood.

I continue seeing Tommy in therapy, knowing it was possible that at least part of his anxiety and OCD symptoms were related to the sexual abuse he experienced. Many of these symptoms have subsided with therapy and the ability to talk openly about his molestation at the bowling alley. If he carried any guilt or shame about the incident, his ability to share the information and be believed by an adult would greatly alleviate his anxiety. Having a mom who listened, empathized and took action was clearly a healing step for Tommy.

I use the radKids[16] training model to educate children about sexual abuse. radKids, Inc. is dedicated to providing proven and effective lifesaving skills for children by teaching them how to "**R**esist **A**ggression **D**efensively." The four major points of radKids are:

---

16 www.radKIDS.org

1. If anyone touches you in a way that makes you uncomfortable, it's okay to say **NO**.

2. If they tell you bad things will happen if you tell, don't believe them, it's a **TRICK**.

3. If they tell you to keep it secret, **DON'T**. Secrets that make you feel bad inside are the ones you need to share.

4. If you tell someone and they don't believe you or don't help, you need to **KEEP TELLING** until you find someone who does, because it's **NOT** Your Fault.

What should parents do if a child discloses sexual abuse? The following are suggestions from The National Child Traumatic Stress Network.[17, 18]

1. **Stay Calm.** Hearing your child has been abused can bring up powerful emotions, but if you become upset, angry, or out of control, this will only make it more difficult for your child to disclose.

2. **Believe** your child, and let your child know he or she is not to blame for what happened. Praise your child for being brave and telling about the sexual abuse.

3. **Protect** your child by getting him or her away from the abuse and immediately reporting the abuse to local authorities.

If you are not sure who to contact, call the ChildHelp National Child Abuse Hotline at

1-800.4.A.CHILD (1-800-422-4453)
http://www.childhelp.org/gethelp

4. **Get Help.** In addition to getting medical care to address any physical damage your child may have suffered (including sexually transmitted diseases), it's important that your child have an opportunity to talk with a mental health professional who specializes in child sexual abuse. Therapy has been shown to successfully reduce distress in families and the effects of sexual abuse on children. For a state-by-state listing of Children's Advocacy Centers, visit the website of the National Children's Alliance.
(http://www.nca.online.org/pages/page.asp?pageid3999).

---

17 The National Child Traumatic Stress Network, *Coping with the Shock of Intrafamilial Sexual Abuse. Information for Parents and Caregivers.*(2009) www.NCTSN.org

---

18 The National Child Traumatic Stress Network, *What to Do If Your Child Discloses Sexual Abuse.* (2009) www.NCTSN.org

5. **Reassure** your child that he or she is loved, accepted, and an important family member. Don't make promises you can't keep (such as saying you won't tell anyone about the abuse), but let your child know you will do everything in your power to protect him or her from harm.

6. **Keep your child informed** about what will happen next, particularly with regard to legal actions. For more information on helping abused children cope with the stress of dealing with the legal system, see the National Child Traumatic Stress Network's factsheet, *Child Sexual Abuse: Coping with the Emotional Stress of the Legal System*, available on the website; http://nctsn.org/nctsnassets/pdfs/caring/emotionalimpactoflegalsystem.pdf.

Chapter 27
Parenting a Heroin Addict: The Difficult Choice
Patricia

IN OUR SOCIETY, addiction strikes every socioeconomic class, race, religion, and culture. It is a struggle for almost every family in some way. At least a third of my clients list substance abuse as one of their most significant problems, either in their own lives or with a family member. The standard addictions we encounter include:

- alcoholism (10% of population)
- gambling (6% of population).
- smoking cigarettes
- overspending or shopaholics
- workaholics
- exercise addiction to the point of anorexia
- overeaters
- sexual addiction
- prescription medication addiction, such as to amphetamines, Vicodin, Oxycontin, Xanax, and Ativan
- other substance addictions, including marijuana, methamphetamine, heroin, cocaine, and crack cocaine.

Of course, the list goes on and on. The problem of heroin addiction and heroin overdose has reached epidemic proportions in many areas of the United States—often in rural towns. In my neighboring state of Vermont, the governor identified heroin as the number one issue in his State of Vermont address in 2014. To quote Governor Peter Shumlin, "What started as an Oxycontin and prescription drug addiction problem in Vermont has now grown into a full-blown heroin crisis."[19] He went on to say that due to Vermont's proximity to Boston, New York, Philadelphia and other cities where heroin is cheap, dealers can make money in Vermont. For example, a $6 bag of heroin purchased in New York City can bring up to $30 in Vermont.

Heroin addicted clients have told me they can buy a bag of heroin for $10 in a park about 10 miles from my office. They say this is cheaper than buying Oxycontin or Vicodin (the opiate prescription equivalents to heroin) on the streets.

This is the story of an ordinary mother who has struggled with her daughter's drug abuse for nearly twenty years and the difficult choices she made along the way regarding her daughter's choices and her daughter's role in her life.

Nicky came to see me in therapy after her former psychiatrist retired. For clinicians this can be a difficult transition, as clients often have trouble forming a strong clinical alliance with a new therapist—especially if they've spent many years with their original therapist. I was aware of this and proceeded slowly with Nicky, letting her take the lead in talking about her life and why she chose me as her new psychologist. Her former therapist referred her to me because she thought we had similar therapeutic styles and felt Nicky would make a satisfactory transition. Fortunately, we did create a healthy therapeutic alliance and so began our journey together, through twenty years of pain, turmoil, and finally acknowledgement and acceptance of the tragedy of heroin addiction.

Nicky is a muscular, buxom woman of average stature who dresses to accentuate her figure and proudly shows her assets. She acknowledges she likes attention from men because she was always the "black sheep" in her family and rarely felt attended to by her mother. Her parents divorced when she was young and she always needed a boyfriend to feel good about herself. She married young to get out of the house and divorced within a year because her first husband was abusive and alcoholic. She fell in love again and married a man she loved. They had two girls together. Nicky says her two girls were her joy and reason to live. Her second husband was also an alcoholic and non-loving toward her and the girls. He was a good financial provider, so she felt stuck in the marriage in order to keep a roof above her head and food on the table.

Nicky had several episodes of major depression and was hospitalized after a suicide attempt with prescription drugs. After this she began therapeutic treatment and started putting her life together. Nicky began cleaning houses to earn money and started saving in order to leave the marriage. With child support and her weekly cleaning jobs, Nicky was able to start out on her own. When her daughters were in their early teens she married her third husband, Paul, whom she calls "the love of my life." He was a hard worker and tried to help Nicky raise

---

19   www.Governor.vermont.gov (State of the State Address, January, 2014)

her daughters. One daughter, Karyn, was "straight and narrow" and never caused Nicky any problems. The other daughter was always a rebel.

Annie, the rebellious daughter, started drinking as a young teen and was soon smoking marijuana and scouring the cabinets for prescription drugs to mix as drug cocktails. Although she was a smart girl, her drug use impeded her academics and she dropped out of high school. Annie worked as a waitress or at odd jobs and lived in Nicky's condominium basement. During this time Nicky began finding empty packets and needles in her basement, stashed under the bed or behind dressers. When confronted about the drug paraphernalia, Annie always lied and lashed out in anger at her mother. Also around this time, Nicky noticed money missing from her wallet and jewelry missing from her jewelry box. She realized Annie was stealing to feed her drug habit. Nicky didn't know where to turn, and this is when she entered treatment with me.

I realized at the onset that Nicky was in a codependent relationship with Annie—a relationship where she tried to set house rules and limits, yet was caught between the rock and the hard place so many parents of addicts must deal with. Should she tell Annie at nineteen years of age to leave the house, knowing full well this would put her on the streets and in danger of prostitution and death by overdose? Or should she let Annie live in a safe home environment even though Annie lied and stole from her?

This was the question she wrestled with for months and years as Annie went through rehabilitation attempts at mental health treatment facilities. Nicky attended Nar-Anon to get guidance from other parents. Annie sporadically went to counseling, but her drug abuse continued and Nicky still found needles and empty drug packets. Paul tried to be supportive, but his patience wore thin when they returned from a trip to find their lovely condominium trashed by drug parties. Annie had finally pushed Nicky to her limit, and Nicky told her to leave. This was fifteen years ago, and the trials and tribulations of tough love have been present in our therapeutic work since then.

I lost touch with Nicky for about eight years when she and her husband moved to Georgia for his work. She would call me on occasion to let me know how she was doing, and relate Annie's whereabouts. I recommended that Nicky find a therapist in Georgia who would help her keep boundaries with Annie, and Nicky wisely did so. During her years in Georgia, Annie was put in rehab several times and also acquired a hepatitis C diagnosis.

Nicky would ask me, "What comes next?"

When I queried, "What do you think is next?"

She would sigh and say, "Annie's overdose." She was beginning to acknowledge that when you have a heroin addicted child you may bury that child someday. Sometimes the word "accept" is used to describe this, but most parents I work with vehemently oppose this term, as they never want to "accept" this; but they are able to "acknowledge" it is reality. This acknowledgement allows them to acquire some kind of distance and detachment.

About five years ago, Nicky returned to therapy when she moved back to New England to a neighboring state. I was happy to hear Annie was still alive and living in subsidized housing for people with mental health diagnoses. Annie had a dual diagnosis of substance abuse and schizoaffective disorder. She was receiving services from the Department of Mental Health in her state and was in counseling for substance abuse and mental illness. Nicky lived across the state and would visit Annie once a month or so, and they spoke on the phone every day.

All seemed to be going well, and then Annie got pregnant. Nicky was ambivalent about this, even though she wanted to be a grandmother. Her other daughter, Karyn, had just divorced and didn't have children from her marriage. Nicky was concerned that Annie would not be able to parent a child, because she still drank heavily and had psychotic episodes.

Nicky told me in one session, "I'm not going to see this baby. I don't want to be a part of this, and end up having to raise Annie's child."

I cautioned her to wait and see how she felt after the baby was born. Nicky was relieved to learn that a social service team in Annie's region was very involved with Annie's condition and pregnancy and closely monitoring the situation. After the baby girl, Chloe, was born, it was clear during the hospital stay that Annie couldn't care for the infant. She didn't want to feed the baby and was more concerned about getting her pain medication than looking after her new daughter. It was also clear that Nicky couldn't stay away and wanted to meet her granddaughter.

The Department of Social Services stepped in, looking for next of kin who would take the infant. At sixty years of age, Nicky didn't want that responsibility, and her daughter Karyn was estranged from her sister and wanted nothing to do with her baby.

This was a difficult choice for Nicky, for she felt she and her husband couldn't raise a child at their ages. A foster/adoptive home was found with a wonderful couple who couldn't conceive their own child. They agreed to let Annie and Nicky visit the baby on weekends at their house. Nicky was relieved and thought the foster family was wonderful.

As months passed, the court case related to adoption was looming. It would be necessary to terminate Annie's parental rights before the baby could be adopted by her foster family. Nicky would be a key witness in this court case. Again, she had another difficult choice to make regarding Annie. Nicky knew that the baby was better off with the foster family than with her daughter, yet she also knew Annie would be livid with her for testifying against her. Nicky knew this could be the end of visits with her granddaughter and the end of her relationship with Annie. But, she had to choose what was best for this innocent child.

She chose to testify that her daughter could not adequately parent Chloe and she supported the decision to terminate parental rights and start the adoption proceedings with the foster family. Annie reacted by vehemently swearing at her mother in the court room and throwing things. But in time, as always, Annie realized her mother was her only support person; the person who'd been with her through thick and thin. Their relationship resumed and the foster family was grateful to Nicky for being involved as a grandmother in their daughter's life.

Ironically, but common in many adoption situations, the adoptive mom became pregnant within months of adopting Nicky's granddaughter. The beautiful granddaughter now has a sister. And Nicky's daughter Karyn remarried and added another lovely girl to the family.

Nicky, who went through hell and back, is now the proud grandmother of three granddaughters and has a relationship with both daughters. She hopes that in time her daughters will reconcile and form a deeper friendship, but for now Nicky is content to host family gatherings that include the extended adoptive family and her daughters and their families. She recently hosted a birthday party for twenty-four "family" members at her house for her three year old granddaughter, Chloe, and her one year old sister. Nicky says with tears in her eyes, "It doesn't get much better than this."

I nod in total agreement.

Unfortunately, just last week I had a session with Nicky and she told me that Annie wasn't consistent in attending her Suboxone clinic and was dropped from the program. Annie quickly returned to the streets and stared getting "dirty urines." Over the Christmas holidays Nicky didn't see Annie, which is the pattern when Annie starts using street drugs. A week after Christmas, Nicky received a frantic call from Annie saying her "boyfriend" had overdosed and was in an induced coma in intensive care. Somehow he miraculously survived, but Nicky said it totally "freaked" her out. Nicky is back on the roller coaster ride of wondering if every call she receives might be telling her Annie has overdosed.

She asked me in our last session, "What would you say to me, Dr. Martin, if I called and told you Annie had died of an overdose?"

I sadly paused and thought for a minute before responding. "I would first ask how you're doing. Then I would reassure you that you've done everything you possibly could to try and keep your daughter alive. I would remind you that you've been a very good mother."

She looked at me and said, "Thank you, I need to know that someone knows that."

I then asked Nicky, "Who do you think will be devastated if Annie does overdose?"

It was Nicky's turn to sadly pause, and after a moment, answer, "Me. Only me."

We both looked at each other knowingly and I nodded in agreement one more time.

Resources:

www.alcoholaddiction.info.org
www.drugabuse.gov
www.Nar-Anon.org

Chapter 28

Transgender Issues: My Daughter Wants to Be My Son

Patricia

WHAT CAN I SAY when a mother tells me, "My daughter wants to become my son!"

Transgender identity issues are a huge challenge for parents and something we rarely discussed openly until recent years.

As the parent of three daughters and a son, I've often wondered how I would deal with learning one of my children was gay or transgender. In order to empathize with my clients I intentionally and purposefully try to put myself in their shoes. I know I can't feel exactly what they're feeling, but I try to understand. I've learned from many clients that reaching understanding and acceptance of a child's sexual and gender orientation may take years, if not decades. But the parents who get past resentment and denial find a deep love that prevails, along with the realization that whatever a child's sexual or gender orientation may be, they are "always our children."

I recently met Jenny, whose daughter wished to change from female to male. Jenny was distraught because her daughter Olivia wanted to change her name to Thomas and was considering undergoing hormonal therapy to begin the process of becoming male. Jenny, who owns and manages a hair salon, wanted to try and understand what went wrong with her parenting that would make her daughter, a freshman in college, want to become her son. Jenny assumed her parenting caused this to happen. Like many parents, she readily took on the burden of responsibility and guilt. Her emotions ranged from anger, to guilt, sadness, frustration, and denial. The stages a parent goes through when they learn a child is "gay" or "trans" are similar to the stages of grief Kubler-Ross described in her classic book, *On Death and Dying*.[20] In essence, hearing your child is transgender sets up a grieving process. The stages of:

- denial,
- anger,
- bargaining,
- depression, and
- acceptance and hope

These stages will come and go throughout the course of grieving.

Having a daughter tell you she wants to become a male can feel like a death of your daughter. Jenny said with tears in her eyes, "I am grieving the daughter I thought I had; the one who would marry someday, wear a wedding gown, have children and come visit me with her husband and my grandchildren."

Now, Jenny is trying to adjust to her daughter becoming her son. He will look different, wear his hair short and masculine, have a deeper voice, dress in men's clothing, and date women. He will want her to call him Thomas rather than the name Olivia, which she selected nineteen years ago. He will bring home girlfriends rather than boyfriends. How could she handle this? Jenny was afraid she might not be able to turn this corner, and even more frightened her husband John, a successful businessman, would never accept Olivia's choice. He was conservative in his beliefs and was a "man's man."

Jenny and John had a younger daughter, Sophie, who was very feminine in her appearance and interests. Jenny worried Olivia would be rejected by her father, and was concerned that Olivia/Thomas would create a split within the family.

Jenny wanted me to meet Olivia. Although she didn't say it in so many words, I knew she hoped I would "talk some sense" into Olivia. I've been asked to do the "come to your senses" interview in the past regarding transgender and sexual orientation decisions. I always tell the parents I will not try to dissuade a young adult from identity exploration. I may recommend counseling and suggest the person spend a year exploring this huge decision before doing anything that can't be reversed, but I will never tell someone who they should become. I told Jenny I thought it best for Olivia to have her own therapist, but I would meet with Olivia for a session or two in order to assist Jenny in her therapy.

Olivia agreed to speak with me "if you think it will help Mom in any way get where I'm coming from." I was curious what Olivia would look like and wondered what she'd tell me about her transgender decision making process.

When I opened the therapy room door to greet Olivia in my waiting room, I was surprised to see a person who looked much younger than her nineteen years. She wore a winter ski cap with bright stripes over her short cropped reddish-brown

---

20   Kubler-Ross, Elisabeth, *On Death and Dying,* 1970, Macmillan Publishing, New York.

hair and had on a pair of Doc Martens black hiking boots, jeans, and a hooded sweatshirt. She could easily have been a pre-adolescent boy. As I got to know Olivia I saw that, although she was intellectually bright, she was still immature in her social-emotional development. She told me she'd never had many friends growing up and always felt different than the other kids. She didn't understand the ins and outs of social communication and always felt left out. Going off to college was a chance to make new friends, but she still didn't find a real niche. She started attending Comicon conferences where people dress like different characters, such as Harry Potter, Hermione Granger, or Star Trek characters, or in her case, Dr. Who, a television character. At these gatherings she began to "feel like herself." She said she realized she preferred dressing like a boy and felt comfortable in this role.

I made a note to myself to explore more about girls and women who have Asperger's syndrome. Many of the characteristics Olivia was describing had the feel of an Asperger's diagnosis. But after one session I wasn't making a diagnosis, rather just tucking an impression into my mind to further explore.

I thanked Olivia for her willingness to meet me and encouraged her to explore therapy with a counselor at college. I asked her to please continue discovering all the areas of identity formation adolescents and young adults typically explore, from work choices, to social identity, to peer choices, to sexual and gender identity. I told Olivia in due time all of these components of identity would begin fitting together for her, but it would take time and exploration. She thanked me, and said, "I hope you can help my Mom understand."

When I next saw Jenny, my first words were to tell her how much I enjoyed my conversation with Olivia. I also informed her I advised Olivia to follow up with counseling at college and take her time addressing the many areas of identity development. I encouraged Jenny to further read about gender identity and connect with other parents who are addressing such issues.

There are national groups for parents called PFLAG (Parents, Families and Friends of Lesbians and Gays). Their website (www.pflag.org) addresses transgender issues as well. Another website for Catholic parents is called Fortunate Families (www.fortunatefamilies.com).

Jenny agreed she needed to find other parents who were experiencing such issues. She reached out to these groups and has been attending on a regular basis. She is beginning to feel less alone and the group members have helped her with this process, which will take years. Jenny hopes in time her husband will attend meetings with her, but she realizes she has to come to terms with this in her own way, even if her husband never does the work. She has vowed that no matter what Olivia/Thomas decides to do, she will always be a loving, accepting mother. She knows her child will need her!

NOTES:

During thirty years of practicing psychotherapy I've witnessed changes in identity formation issues that surround career choices, religious identity, social identity, sexual orientation, and now gender identity. Years ago, people worried about ethnic identity. I recall one story from the 1940s about parents who forbade their Irish daughter from marrying the Italian man she loved. This woman abided her parent's wishes and never married, instead living her life as caretaker for her parents into their dotage. I've had clients relate stories of elopement because their parents didn't accept their love of someone who was from a different social class. (Delores's story in Chapter Nineteen).

I listen to stories of families who prevent interfaith marriages by forbidding a Catholic daughter from marrying her Jewish boyfriend, or their Christian son marrying a Muslim. In 1967 the inter-racial dating issue was presented in the movie *Guess Who's Coming to Dinner*. In the 1970s and 1980s the issues were more about women's liberation and sexual identity. Parents adjusted to young women marrying and not changing their surnames. The gay rights movement created further questions and angst for parents related to a child's "coming out" and dating and marrying same sex partners. Some of these concerns still linger for many parents.

Now, in the new millennium we face issues of gender identity. In contrast to sexual identity, which defines one's sexual preference (heterosexual, homosexual, bisexual, asexual), gender identity defines whether one considers oneself male or female. Transgender is an umbrella term for any gender identity that differs from the one associated with the sex assigned at birth.

In addition we now have a third gender labeled "genderqueer" that falls outside the male/female binary. This third gender reflects not feeling accurately labeled as either male or female. These new movements create issues many parents will face in the future. The LGBTQ (Lesbian, Gay, Bisexual, Transgender, Questioning) movement is becoming more prevalent each year. Sometimes a transgender person will choose to dress and style themselves as the opposite sex. Others go through changing their bodies hormonally or surgically to align with an internal gender identity.

Over the years I've watched sexual orientation become more mainstream and seen more parents who are open and willing to love their children, no matter what. This isn't easy, and I marvel at the deep love these parents have for their children.

Resources:

www.pflag.org
www.fortunatefamilies.com
www.apa.org (American Psychological Association website, under Topics: LGBT)

Chapter 29
The Warrior Mom: Staying Alive For the Children
Patricia

AS A PSYCHOLOGIST I often work with clients who are struggling with a cancer diagnosis. Cancer touches almost every life in some way or another, yet many people diagnosed with this devastating disease manage to fight hard and overcome the odds. I've known clients who beat the disease by having a strong will to live, an optimistic attitude, and refusing to give up. One such person is my client Samantha. I call her Warrior Mom because she has fought every day—for five years now—to stay alive for her young sons. Her determination, tenacity, spirit, and positive attitude have inspired me, and I share her story in hopes it will give you courage to face obstacles in your life.

Samantha came to therapy after a nasty fight with her husband that she feared might be the beginning of divorce. In the first session I usually gather relevant background information on the client, and this time I was floored to hear what had transpired for this forty year old mother of two young boys. During the previous six years Samantha had a miscarriage, delivered her first son via C-section, had a second son seventeen months later via C-section, had a painful lump in her right breast biopsied and was diagnosed with aggressive triple negative breast cancer while her sons were seventeen and thirty-four months old. She underwent a double mastectomy two weeks after the diagnosis, then had temporary breast implants and the removal of thirteen lymph nodes (three positive for cancer). She began chemotherapy on her oldest son's third birthday (dose dense ACT) and continued chemotherapy for three and a half months. Then she had surgery to replace breast expanders with saline implants, and later had repair surgery to replace a leaking implant.

Within a month of this time Samantha felt a painful lump in the same spot as the original tumor. Samantha knew from experience that cancerous lumps usually are not painful, so she was optimistic and the doctors assured her it was probably tender scar tissue. But the lump was biopsied and she received a second breast cancer diagnosis in less than a year. The lump was removed and radiation began, but was stopped when Samantha felt another painful lump which was biopsied and found to be noncancerous. She restarted radiation for another month. When radiation was complete, Samantha had reconstructive surgery on her left breast to replace the implant.

Three months later Samantha was cleared to exercise again. Always a health nut and exercise queen, Samantha felt she was returning to normalcy. Then a month later a spot on her nose was biopsied and found to be basal cell skin cancer, which was treated with a surgical procedure. Four months after this Samantha entered therapy with me following the fight with her husband.

After Samantha gave me this six year history, all I could say was, "WOW!" She laughed and said, "People do what they have to do, Dr. Martin."

Within a month of our first session, Samantha's husband Larry filed for divorce. I had the feeling her husband never really accepted the fact that his wife had cancer and was going through difficult treatments. Although I didn't meet him, I recommended they try couples therapy. He refused therapy as he had over the years, and the divorce proceeded. This was a contentious divorce battle, with the two of them living in the same house until after the divorce trial. Custody issues were raised and a Guardian Ad Litem was hired to help the court determine custody. After a year and a half battle the divorce became final. Samantha obtained physical custody of her boys and shared legal custody with Larry.

Finally, Samantha could breathe easier. But three days after the divorce was final she was rushed to the emergency room and admitted to the hospital with her neck grossly swollen and bulging. The doctors found a tumor in Samantha's lung that caused her lymph nodes to swell, leading to a 75% blockage of her Superior Vena Cava, the large blood vessel draining blood from the head to the heart. Called SVC syndrome, this condition is dangerous.

The results of tests were inconclusive, so the doctors treated it as a separate lung cancer. One doctor told Samantha, "This is not good. I'll have to bring you as close to death as I can before bringing you back."

Samantha received seven weeks of daily radiation and chemo at the same time. As a single mom, Monday through Friday, her days consisted of waking up, taking the kids to school, getting a ride for the two hour drive to Boston for radiation/chemo treatment, getting a ride home for the two hour trip, and picking up the kids from school in the afternoon. Samantha was exhausted and sick from the treatments she described as "grueling." At one point she had an allergic reaction to the chemo drug and couldn't breathe. Sometimes she stayed in the hospital overnight for her treatments.

At the end of the seven week radiation regimen, her husband announced he was going to seek full custody of the children because of her new cancer diagnosis. Samantha contacted her attorney and the judge dismissed the request. Samantha's lawyer wrote an article about this case for "The Healthcare News" law section. In her article she states,

> Trying to use a disease or medical condition against your co-parent will only show you don't have your children's best interest in mind. A judge will likely believe that, if a parent is so sick that they can potentially die, it is critical for children to spend as much time as possible with the sick parent to deal with the impending future.

The article basically stated that custody should not be changed due to cancer or other medical diagnoses and was a scathing criticism of any parent who would stoop so low.

The saga continued as eight months later Samantha found a lump inside her eye and the doctor recommended surgical removal. Fortunately, this lump was not cancerous. Within a month of the eye surgery, Samantha noticed a wound on her breast in the same spot as the original tumor. A biopsy produced the third diagnosis of breast cancer and the doctors corrected their earlier diagnosis of lung cancer—the new diagnosis was stage four breast cancer with metastasis to the lung.

Samantha was only forty-five and her boys were six and seven years old. She told me she had to beat this for her sons. She could not give up. She would keep fighting, no matter what. I told her I would pray for her and gave her a special wooden disc prayer wheel that had belonged to my dear, recently deceased father. I told her my dad would be her angel and watch out for her.

She said, "You know, Dr. Martin, I'm not very religious, but I do believe in the power of prayer. So thank you so much."

Again, I told Samantha it was my honor to be with her on this journey.

She waited through the Christmas holiday and in the new year Samantha had surgery to remove the breast cancer lump. Conventional chemotherapy was no longer a logical option because Samantha's cancer had quickly returned after both chemo treatments, so the physicians tested her tumor to discover whether she was eligible for treatment with a new trial chemo drug. Samantha waited, praying she would be a candidate, knowing she'd try whatever they threw at her in order to stay alive for her boys. She met the criteria and was eligible—her cancer had the right markers and she could begin the new treatment, which was probably her last chance for survival.

The new cancer drug required infusions every three weeks for a year. The doctors told her this drug had some success with melanoma patients, but she was only the twelfth breast cancer patient in the country to try it. The drug was working for five of the other eleven patients and Samantha hoped to be the sixth. After three months of treatment, based on a CT scan, the pharmaceutical company conducting the trial determined the drug wasn't working for Samantha and she should stop taking it. Her doctor believed otherwise. She convinced Samantha to stay on the drug and argued her case with the pharmaceutical firm. Her next CT scan showed a thirty percent reduction in the tumor; her doctor was right, the new drug was working.

Samantha told me her doctor entered the treatment room with tears in her eyes the day she told her. At first she thought the tears meant bad news, but her doctor said "I always cry when I have good news like this to share."

The next scan six weeks later showed a forty percent reduction. Just today, in October, Breast Cancer Awareness Month, I received a text from Samantha saying:

"The tumor is now seventy-five percent smaller than when I started this drug! And the amazing part is I feel relatively well. Of course I'm tired, my lung is permanently damaged from radiation, I have headaches almost every single day, blah, blah, blah, but that's to be expected after everything my body has been through over the last five years. It's all good!"

These are the moments as a therapist when I breathe a sigh of relief and cry.

Yep, I sit at the desk in my office reading a text and begin to cry. I let it flow because I know I need to let myself feel this moment. I am so relieved and grateful that Samantha has made it through another scan. I text back to her in bold faced type, "HURRAH! GO CELEBRATE!"

I thought of Samantha's beloved sons, thankful to know she'd remain part of their lives. Through all the bad things that happened to her, Samantha's gift to them was a normal, happy childhood with a loving mother. At several points she had to decide what to tell her sons. Should she let them know she was battling cancer? She asked me to share her thoughts about this decision:

"Because my children were only eighteen months and thirty-four months old when I was first diagnosed with breast cancer, I chose not to use the "C" word with my boys. Obviously I had to tell them the doctors gave me medicine that made me lose my hair. But, I never let them see me sick, nor did I ever tell them that I was too sick to play. In the middle of winter I would be building snowmen in the yard with them, go inside the house to vomit, and return to play. I had to hold my breath a couple of months ago when someone was talking about cancer in front of my boys.

One of my boys interrupted the person and asked, 'What's cancer' and the other said, 'Yeah, what is it?'

I felt such a sense of relief that I've been able to protect my sons from the fear and uncertainty that come with cancer. Not everyone will agree with my decision to keep this from them, but I deeply believe young children need to play, have fun, and feel comfort in believing their parents will take care of them."

And that's exactly what this Warrior Mom continues to do.

Cancer Statistics:

In 2014, approximately 1.7 million new cases of cancer were diagnosed and over five hundred thousand people died from cancer. This devastating illness remains the second most common cause of death in the United States, accounting for nearly one of every four deaths.

The lifetime probability of developing some form of cancer is 44% in men and 38% in women. The death rate is most significant for lung, bronchial, and breast cancer in women in the United States. One of every eight women in this country will develop breast cancer, while one of every 16 will be diagnosed with lung or bronchial cancer. These statistics provided by the American Cancer Society are staggering. Yet as overwhelming and confounding as the numbers sound, millions of people are fighting and overcoming cancer with the help of new treatments and early diagnosis.

Resources:

www.m.cancer.org/
www.acor.org/
www.cancersupportcommunity.org
www.bcrc.org/
City of Hope: Breast Cancer Awareness

Chapter 30
Grandparent's Rights: A Grandmother Fights On
Patricia

RIGHT AWAY I KNEW I was in for an exhilarating ride when Carol Ann bounded into my office ten years ago. She was a petite redhead with a short, spiky haircut accentuated by bright, dangling earrings. She shook my hand vigorously and blurted out, "I've never been to therapy before, Dr. Martin, and I'm not sure you can help me, but I think I need to be here."

Boy, oh boy, that was an understatement! I soon understood Carol Ann was going through hell and high water, but in the end her journey was rewarding and successful, although marked by tears and anguish along the way. Carol Ann's story of courage and determination will change her family for generations to come. It is first a saga of mother love, and then grandmother love.

Carol Ann came to the office alone, although she said her husband would hear all about our conversation through her. During ten years of therapy I don't think Carol Ann ever actually relaxed and sat back on my therapy couch. Instead she always perched on the edge of the seat, her hands folded and her eyes bright and wide. She had much to share with me and didn't want to forget a word. She wanted to make sure I absorbed every morsel of what she was feeding me throughout our journey together.

Carol Ann's first statement during our initial session related the death of her oldest daughter Sandi, eight months earlier. This was a sad tale of how her twenty-four year old daughter, an avid equestrian, was dragged by a horse on a trail and hit her head on a rock. Sandi died instantly, with her husband and sister right behind her on the trail. She left a twenty month old daughter, Kaitlin, who was doted on by the entire family.

Carol Ann had always promised her daughter she would take care of Kaitlin if anything happened to Sandi. This sounds strange coming from such a young mother, but Carol Ann believed Sandi had a premonition that she might not live to raise her daughter.

Grief work with parents who've lost a child is among the most difficult challenges a therapist can undertake. I find it especially difficult if the child who has died matches the age of one of my four children, even though that does give me an extra helping of empathy. At the time of her death Sandi was close in age to my oldest daughter. Carol Ann and I bonded almost immediately, perhaps because she saw tears in my eyes when she shared her tale of loss—and because I told her I could only imagine her pain. She felt a kindred spirit in the room, and thus our journey together began.

Carol Ann began healing week by week, month by month. She, her husband, and their surviving daughter formed a tightly knit family. They had memorial events and fundraisers in Sandi's honor. Kaitlin stayed at their home every other weekend and frequently through the week. Kaitlin's father, Ronny, was a farmer and often left her with grandparents during the day, or with her great grandmother when Carol Ann was working. The family had a special bedroom for Kaitlin and she loved visiting them. Although their son-in-law wasn't especially interested in their family activities, he occasionally spent time with his father-in-law.

Carol Ann began worrying if Ronny was able to care for a toddler's needs, so she offered to take Kaitlin whenever her son-in-law needed her. She began seeing Kaitlin dirty and dressed in shabby clothes. The first thing Carol Ann did with each visit was give Kaitlin a fun bubble bath and wash her hair. Carol Ann regularly bought new clothes for her granddaughter to keep up with the growing toddler who needed larger clothes and shoes on a monthly basis. Ronny seemed to appreciate these efforts and expressed gratitude. All seemed to be going well.

Then a woman entered her son-in-law's life and within a few months she and her two children moved in with him. Carol Ann thought this might be a good thing, if the house was cleaned and Kaitlin was better cared for. Just the opposite! Alcohol and drugs entered the scene. This felt terribly disheartening to Carol Ann. She tried to tip-toe around the issues of her slovenly clad granddaughter in hopes of keeping things copacetic between herself and Ronny. Her husband was a great buffer and able to maintain a "good enough" relationship with his son-in-law.

But visits with Kaitlin began to lessen because the girlfriend didn't like Kaitlin leaving her "family" home. Then the next tragedy befell the family. Carol Ann's husband was diagnosed with pancreatic cancer. He courageously battled the disease for eighteen months, with one of his motivating factors the desire to be there for Kaitlin and help Carol Ann traverse the storms that lay ahead. When he died she no longer had a connecting bridge to Ronny, and thus the connection to Kaitlin became more tenuous. The girlfriend was a formidable obstacle.

Carol Ann knew she had a duty to try with all her strength to maintain a relationship with her now five year old granddaughter. She loved Kaitlin and had promised her daughter she would always be in Kaitlin's life. Not only did she, her mother, and her other daughter miss Kaitlin, they also knew Kaitlin mourned for them. Carol Ann tried to stay connected with phone calls to Ronny, but the calls weren't answered. Birthday gifts and cards were returned unopened. She would try and see her granddaughter at school to give her a hug, but this became more difficult when Ronny complained to the school.

At last Carol Ann decided she had to take legal action and explore her rights as a maternal grandmother. All the while I kept advising and counseling Carol Ann to stay the course. I let her know I would help in whatever way I could.

Now the journey became an odyssey similar to great Greek epics, with frequent court battles and heartbreaking obstacles. But Carol Ann never gave up. She would scale any mountain and battle any storm for her granddaughter. She had promised to care for Kaitlin, and she would die trying if necessary.

I tried to help by scheduling a therapy session with Carol Ann and her son-in-law. To my surprise he was willing. But, at the last minute, his fiancée called and said Carol Ann couldn't be there, but she and Ronny would come. They wanted me to know that they were the parents and Carol Ann needed to stop bothering them. I made sure Carol Ann agreed to have me see them without her. She was disappointed, but thought it was a good idea for me to see who they were. (Of course they required that Carol Ann pay for the session).

My session with Ronny and his fiancée gave credence to Carol Ann's concerns. Ronny entered dressed in tattered clothes and dirty boots. He was unshaven and smelled bad. The fiancée wore a tight fitting, low cut shirt, with tight jeans that looked like they took her a day to squeeze into. She wore spiked high heels with a Farah Fawcett type hairdo and chomped on a stick of gum. When we discussed parenting Kaitlin, Ronny seemed clueless, while the fiancée was controlling and inflexible. She interrupted every time Ronny tried to express his opinion, and gave him snide glances if he ever appeared cooperative in his responses to me. I could see a long and painful road lay ahead for Carol Ann in her quest for regular, permanent visits with Kaitlin.

My role throughout the years as Carol Ann's therapist was to support her during this uphill climb. I wrote letters of support for Carol Ann to the courts; I spoke with Department of Child and Family Services workers; I spoke with therapists who were counseling Kaitlin (a group of therapists who'd been counseling the step mother for years). I also spoke to various attorneys Carol Ann hired over the years, advised her in selecting attorneys, and counseled Carol Ann's other daughter who had a tough time missing Kaitlin. I kept in touch with Carol Ann throughout her legal struggles with emails and office visits as needed.

Evidence mounted that pointed to negligent, if not abusive parenting by Kaitlin's father and stepmom. Reports were filed by neighbors and Carol Ann about drunk driving, negligence related to medical care, and unsafe home practices. The reports were explored by the Department of Child and Family Services, but never substantiated enough to require Kaitlin's removal from the home. A case worker stated that a parent had to take "minimal care of a child" and they thought Kaitlin's father was doing that. The department said they thought it was a family feud that needed to be resolved.

With every accusation, Carol Ann moved further away from visitations. Ultimately, she needed legal counsel to fight for grandparent's rights. In one court appeal the judge actually told Carol Ann she no longer had a legal right to stand in his courtroom and fight for legal rights to see Kaitlin because she was no longer the grandmother after the stepmother adopted Kaitlin. This was the first Carol Ann knew of the adoption that, sadly, occurred on Carol Ann's fiftieth birthday. This comment and ruling by the judge devastated Carol Ann, but she didn't give up. She educated herself on stepparent adoptions and believed the judge's decision was an error. She appealed and asked that he be removed from her case.

The exact day her attorney filed the appeal, the stepmom filed false assault and battery charges against Carol Ann. These charges were ultimately thrown out by the clerk magistrate and judge. The court officials knew this was clear retaliation on the stepmom's part and they warned her in court to never try that again. Two years later a decision was handed down from the court of appeals, and the evidence was sufficient to have the former judge removed from the case and all his rulings vacated. This is an unusual occurrence, yet correctly decided, given the emotional harm being done to Kaitlin.

This child, who once had her maternal great grandmother, grandmother, and aunt in her life on a weekly basis hadn't seen her mother's family in over three and a half painful years. During eight months of time awaiting the trial, the stepmother was charged with operating under the influence. A domestic disturbance police report led to Kaitlin being taken to the home of her paternal grandmother.

Finally, after eight years of legal frustration, Carol Ann had her day in court for grandparent's rights. She was on the witness stand for over four and a half hours recalling the last eight years of her life and her relationship with her granddaughter. After a two day trial, Carol Ann won the right to begin seeing her granddaughter.

Two months later she still hadn't seen Kaitlin. She had to file contempt charges because the family wouldn't follow court orders. Six months would pass before Carol Ann was allowed to visit Kaitlin on a regular basis. The judge ordered Ronny and his wife to allow visitation or "suffer the repercussions of the court."

Shortly afterward, Carol Ann learned her son-in-law and his wife had separated after the stepmom was charged with armed home invasion. The stepmom stayed in the house and Kaitlin was now living with her father at his brother's house.

Kaitlin experienced a huge amount of turmoil and emotional negligence during that eight year period, but the visitations finally began. Carol Ann took one visit at a time, hoping the influence of her family would have a positive impact. Now, Kaitlin loves coming to Carol Ann's house and having hot meals, loves the feeling of clean, sweetly smelling sheets at night, and enjoys having a loving grandmother tuck her in at night and say her prayers.

I advised Carol Ann not to focus on things like table manners at this point (Carol Ann was saddened to see Kaitlin eat with her hands and not use utensils), but rather focus on showing Kaitlin she is loved and cared for by her aunt, grandmother, and great grandmother. Right now Kaitlin needs a safe, consistent home she can go to on a regular basis. The grandmother/grandchild relationship will take time as Kaitlin is now ten years of age, but it will happen, and both Kaitlin and Carol Ann will be better for it. I will be available to help and guide them in whatever ways I can through the years ahead.

Carol Ann asked me to share her own words for anyone else who's going through this process:

My relationship with my granddaughter suffered for eight years from the actions taken by her father and stepmother. But I promised my daughter Sandi on the day she passed away that we would forever watch out for, and be there, for my granddaughter. I am left, without my husband, to forever live up to that promise. As my lawyer said, "I am the last man standing!"

My thoughts to anyone attempting this journey are that it will be a long, emotional ride, not to mention the financial strain on you and your family. I have suffered it all, but Kaitlin has suffered more. Even knowing what I know now, I would do it all again. She is worth every single penny of the $130,000.00 we spent. Her father made a decision to think only of himself after the death of her mother, and Kaitlin paid the price. She was his weapon of choice against me and it worked for a while. But ultimately truth came out. I never had any reason to lie in court; the truth was bad enough. If it weren't for the support of family, friends, Dr. Martin, and the community, as well as faith in God, I would not be standing today. The only thing I am guilty of is loving my granddaughter. Even though what has happened to Kaitlin emotionally is a huge challenge for us, we now look forward to our future together."

Resources:

www.lawlib.state.ma.us/subject/about/grandparent.html.
www.nolo.com/legal
www.Grandparents.about.com

Serious Illness

Chapter 31
The Imposter Phenomenon: Calming the Inner Critic
Helene

WHEN I FIRST MET Harlow, she was recently discharged from the emergency psychiatric treatment unit after deliberately slicing her left wrist deeply enough to require stitches. An attractive, stylishly dressed teenager, Harlow had dark hair and sparkling ebony eyes that would eventually twinkle. I would later come to love her broad, impish smile.

At the time of our first meeting she was eighteen years old, a senior in high school, an honor student, and also depressed and angry. She was always on time and polite, but also guarded, a bit irritable, and easily defensive. Although her depression was palpable, her anger caught my attention first. A breakup with a boyfriend precipitated the suicide attempt, but as we continued meeting she gradually revealed the most important sources for her rage.

Harlow's parents met in college: her mother was a white art student, her father an African American business student. Her mother began exhibiting symptoms of mania and psychosis as a young adult. When the marriage ended, Harlow's mom returned to her parents' home with her two small daughters. Her mental health worsened, culminating with dropping off the two little girls on their father's front porch and committing suicide shortly after when Harlow was five years old. Harlow's father William barely knew the girls and clearly knew little about parenting. He had never cared for them for any length of time, leaving that to their now deceased mother and two grandmothers who were loving and attentive. Harlow did develop a close relationship with her maternal grandparents later on and was comforted by her dad's mother, who was very nurturing.

Harlow and her sister Evelyn didn't know William well and he quickly handed over childcare to a series of women who passed through his life. The girls developed no attachment to these women, some of whom were physically abusive to them. One can imagine how the two little girls, both extremely intelligent, developed behavioral issues in response to their chaotic and loss-filled lives. Harlow indicated that supervision was often missing when they were young, leaving them vulnerable to abuse by others as well.

William's parenting style alternated between emotional distance and being an imposing disciplinarian, holding the girls hostage hours at a time with lengthy lectures filled with disappointment and rage. These rants became more frequent during the girls' teenage years. Perhaps he sensed he was losing control of them. He would call them irresponsible, ungrateful, ignorant, and on the road to being losers. Harlow would sit stoically, stone faced, doing her best to tune him out. But William's disparaging, critical words, hit their target—her very soul. They influenced the person she would become and prophesied a life of inner torment, self- loathing, and continuing self-sabotage.

Attention deficit disorder, diagnosed during our first year of working together, complicated Harlow's situation. ADHD can give the impression of carelessness and irresponsibility, which added fuel to her father's critical explosions. Successful students may have ADHD; it has no relationship to intelligence, but can make succeeding in school more difficult. In college Harlow required various accommodations, such as a longer time for tests and extended deadlines for papers.

In high school Harlow thought of suicide, but more often developed cutting behaviors to release her inner rage. Cutters explain that feeling physical pain is preferable to their emotional pain and scars. She always made sure the cuts were hidden by her clothing. Even in adulthood, during times of emotional turmoil an impulse to cut can occur.

Harlow was never close with her sister Evelyn, who became a successful engineer, but wasn't so fortunate in personal relationships. Harlow seemed to develop a comfortable relationship with me. I was conscious of her need for parenting (indeed she and my older daughter are the same age and graduated from high school the same year).

Over the years, Harlow came to me for treatment from time to time as her circumstances changed. She went off to college, but dropped out due to a pregnancy. She had a son, Brendon, and raised him on her own until she met Jake, whom she eventually married. They had two more children and Jake helped raise Brendon as though he were his own. Initially, Jake showed immaturity and seemed to be less responsible than Harlow, but in time he "stepped up" and became the supportive husband and good father the family needed. Harlow experienced times of contentment, but when she decided she wanted to pursue higher education and become the professional she knew she could be, her self-doubt and tendency to self-sabotage emerged again.

Harlow worked as a lab assistant at the medical center and realized she wanted a career in health care. While working part-time and raising her children, she completed a degree at the local community college and finished first in her class. She was accepted to a prestigious nurse practitioner program and graduated after years of self-doubt and self-sabotage.

Over the years, and in spite of her outward progress, Harlow still missed her mother, the woman she feared becoming. The anniversary of her mother's suicide, her mother's birthday, Mother's Day; each of these events could send her into a spiral of bipolar depression. We tried to prepare for these dates by upping her medications or restarting them. Harlow's fear of being like her mother (mentally ill and killing herself) caused her to fight and resist the need to take medication for almost 25 years. When she was younger, she never thought she would live past the age her mother was when she died (30).

Despite her accomplishments, Harlow could never fully escape her inner critic. She never felt good enough or worthy of success, no matter how hard she worked. At times she thought about ending her life. Complicating her situation, ADHD continued to cause Harlow problems in keeping up with paperwork, meeting deadlines, and other issues in her professional life. While I was in awe of her accomplishments despite her traumatic history, multiple losses, bipolar disorder and ADHD, I could sense she still felt inadequate on the inside.

Now over forty years old, Harlow still fights her inner critic. Many people who have accomplished much despite adversity and abuse struggle with feeling worthy of success and must fight against self-sabotaging behavior. Along with feeling unworthy comes the sense of being an imposter—a person who pretends to be someone else.

There are times when Harlow seems to recognize her accomplishments and feel some pride, especially for her three wonderful children. One of Harlow's greatest strengths is the ability to laugh at herself and use that to forge positive relationships with coworkers and patients. Her humor rivals the best stand-up comics as she speaks of situations she encounters at work and home. Her background and love for others makes her a compassionate, empathic, healthcare provider. Hopefully soon, Harlow will no longer need to punish herself or question her authenticity. People who know her realize she is the "real deal."

Imposter Phenomenon: When we're never good enough

A journal article *"The Imposter Phenomenon in High Achieving Women: Dynamics and Therapeutic Intervention"*[21] introduced this concept in 1978. The author, Pauline Rose Clance, Ph. D, continues to study and treat patients

---

21   Clance, Pauline Rose; Imes, Suzanne A.(1978). "The imposter phenomenon in high achieving women: Dynamics and therapeutic intervention." Psychotherapy: Therapy, Research, &Practice 15(3):1

with these issues, which seem to mainly affect high achieving women. Women with multiple degrees and enormous professional accomplishments can have the "internal experience of intellectual phonies."

Interestingly, both women who grew up in families with low expectations for them and those who were greatly valued and expected to achieve success can experience self-doubt and feel like phonies. Worldly successes aren't generally fulfilling. Group therapy of these highly successful "imposters" may be successful in correcting cognitive distortions.

Chapter 32
Multiple Personality Disorder: Making Friends with Rage

Helene

MY TWO O'CLOCK time slot every Thursday was reserved for Doris, a forty-three year old, large, complex, and at times frightening woman who became one of my greatest teachers and made me proud to be her friend over a fifteen year association. Being Doris's friend came with a price: worry, admiration, revulsion, and heartbreak.

I could predict the mood of each session as I watched Doris trudge up the sidewalk and pass my office window, usually exhausted from her day job. The slope of her shoulders, the expression on her face, and the speed of her gait were all predictive of what was to come. Doris often wore large brooches. A particularly striking one was the image of a stalking tiger with claws much like her fingernails: long, menacing, and painted bright red, the color of blood. She revealed her superior intelligence with a vocabulary that reflected her love of reading and a nimble, clever mind.

Doris was a guarded woman. She had been encouraged to get therapy by her primary care physician, Dr. F., when she experienced multiple physical symptoms of stress, including chest pain. She told her doctor about recurring depression and symptoms of posttraumatic stress disorder. He also knew she'd experienced severe abuse as a child.

Over the initial six years of therapy Doris gradually lifted the curtain on her history—the horror she experienced as a child and her efforts to cope as an adult. She had developed what she referred to as a facade to hide her history and vulnerabilities from others, including her children. As she sat in my office, early on I noticed that periodically her expressive blue eyes would look up to the right, rhythmically moving from side to side, and silence would fall in the room. It took me months to figure out she was listening to internal voices during those times. A negative voice would berate her and me and throw doubt on my sincerity. That voice caused Doris enormous distress and held her in a vicelike grip. If she revealed too much to me she would be severely punished when she got home.

Identifying what was going on in these sessions contributed to the diagnosis of multiple personality disorder, or the more current term, dissociative identity disorder. Doris could lose days at a time while her inner selves took over and often quarreled. Rarely, Doris's child part emerged and she would become mute. Her primary care physician (PCP) told me he once found her curled up in the corner of the exam room, inconsolably crying.

As Doris tried to explore her various parts, she found it less threatening to draw pictures. One day she came in with a portfolio of vivid drawings of various cat people. As a child she observed the way cat families behaved, and she learned maternal behavior from them. The cat people represented emotions of various parts of her personality. One was ferocious with dripping blood from its long red claws.

The most difficult sessions for her were to verbalize horrific activities in which she was a victim, or even worse for her (and me), those in which she was the perpetrator. We were both exhausted at the end of those sessions.

Doris had a gentler side as well. She loved her pet cat and when she felt insecure or regressed she kept a tiny stuffed bunny in her purse which peeked out and gave her reassurance during the session. She also had a creative side and made beautiful objects out of silk flowers. I purchased lovely floral wreaths from her over the years. She also loved and admired her oldest daughter and her son and spoke often of their accomplishments. She appreciated classical music, particularly operas that would help her relax.

Six years into treatment, after a particularly lethal suicide attempt, Doris revealed that the angry, abusive part of her which she named Rage had tried to kill her. The murderous part of her had stabbed Doris in the abdomen and seemed to have no concept that Doris's death would be his as well. Over time it became clear that Rage developed to protect her as a child. Following that revelation, I suggested the goal of treatment might be altered from integrating or destroying negative aspects of her personality to improving communication and empathy among the parts. She gradually was able to speak for all the aspects of her personality in session: "We don't want to be here today."

She was able to recall the tremendous abuse she experienced by her mother, including getting electrical shocks. Earlier in treatment she could communicate that event only in drawings. One can suspect some of the abuse occurred when she was very young—preverbal—which made discussing it verbally impossible.

Around this time in her treatment I gave Doris a small picture book by Terry Cooper called *Accepting the Troll under the Bridge*[22] in an effort to make the negative and angry parts of her less frightening. It took three more years of therapy for her to finally begin reading the book. At that time Doris said, "I only trust you and Dr. F."

Dr. F. and I spoke on the phone at times because we both sincerely cared for Doris and worried for her safety. Doris struggled with a constant internal battle over taking insulin, and her body deteriorated from the complications of diabetes and a life full of stress, hard work, and mistreatment.

Two years before her death she began to further identify the various aspects of herself through inner communication. I struggled with trying to win trust and make alliances. Doris's eyes would change when Rage was present. She would look at me with the cold glassy stare of a wolf. Despite Doris' size and learning of her frightening behavior in the past and murderous thoughts toward her husband who had betrayed her, ("Just listening to him breathe makes me want to get a knife"), I personally never felt any fear of her. I did feel apprehension before sessions I knew would be difficult. Doris was one of the most challenging patients I have ever worked with.

She caused me to worry about her safety and the safety of her husband for whom she had mixed feelings. Her times of wishing him dead alternated with a sense of gratitude for how he provided a safe family for her three daughters. Once, after a particularly worrisome time, I shared my concern with Doris: "I worry that you could hurt yourself or your husband and get into a lot of trouble" to which she curtly replied, "I don't need a therapist who worries about me." Enough said.

Doris started taking painkillers about two years before her death to ease back pain, neuropathy, and abdominal pain. She battled with her weight, which contributed to her discomfort and out of control diabetes.

My last meeting with Doris was eventful; she came in beautifully dressed and made up, wearing one of her trademark hats. I like to think that somehow she knew this would be our last visit and she wanted me to remember her looking well. Her physical health rapidly declined during the next few weeks and she fell into a coma and was transferred from ICU to a palliative care unit where she ultimately died, never awakening.

I think of her to this day—particularly when I look at her beautiful wreath that still hangs in my office. Writing this chapter has reminded me of the stress involved in caring and being responsible for Doris, but it also reminds me of my gratitude that she allowed me into her life—a rare and incredible privilege—and for teaching me how to identify dissociative disorders in other patients. And

---

22   Cooper, Terry D. *Accepting the Troll Underneath the Bridge: Overcoming Our Self-Doubts*. Eugene: Wipf & Stock Pub., 2010.

as I write these words, while listening to a beautiful adagio Doris would have appreciated, my eyes well up with tears, and I realize I still grieve for her.

In my initial evaluation of Doris, I noted she had the following goals for treatment:

to be less paranoid in interacting with others,

to have peace,

to have a friend.

Knowing I may have helped her bravely accomplish all those goals before she passed away gives me a sense of calm. I hope Doris has found the peace she never had while living and I also hope she would approve of this chapter, which honors her life, struggles, and accomplishments.

What is Posttraumatic Stress Disorder (PTSD)?

Posttraumatic stress disorder is classified as a Trauma and Stressor-Related Disorder in the *DSM-5*. The trauma or stress experienced must be of an extraordinary nature and often indicates the person or loved one's life was endangered. A person with PTSD can't get away from the event and may have recurring nightmares or flashbacks in which it is re-experienced over and over again with all the original emotional distress. The person may avoid exposure to anything that reminds him or her of the event and become chronically on alert. Doris protected herself from awful memories by compartmentalizing the traumatic events and emotions. When she did allow memories to come forward in therapy, it was as though she relived them on the spot. It's easy to see why patients with severe trauma histories will avoid therapy in fear of being swallowed up again by these events. Doris's dependence on alcohol as a young woman was one way for her to suppress memories. People with PTSD often struggle with substance abuse. Think of the tragedy of all our homeless veterans who struggle with drugs and alcohol.

Combat veterans often suffer with PTSD, as do victims of other violent acts, like Doris. Antidepressant medications, antianxiety medications, and sleep aids as well as mood stabilizers can be helpful to manage the symptoms.

What is Dissociation?

Dissociation is a term describing a splitting from conscious awareness memories, feelings, and/or perceptions that cannot be voluntarily recalled. It is a psychological defense against painful thoughts and recollections.[23] The *DSM-5* lists Dissociative Identity Disorder, Dissociative Amnesia, and Depersonalization/Derealization

---

23   Ayc, Frank J., Jr, *Lexicon of Psychiatry, Neurology, and the Neurosciences*, Baltimore. Williams & Wilkins, 1995, 216.

Disorder as Dissociative Disorders.[24] Depersonalization and/or derealization can occur in relatively normal people under stressful situations. People speak of feeling outside of themselves or of feeling as though nothing is real.

I have witnessed dissociative amnesia in the emergency room when a mother couldn't accept that her child had died. It was as though her brain refused to comprehend the events and what was to come. She left under the watchful eyes of close relatives, and I shudder at the thought of what that poor woman went through when reality finally entered her consciousness. She was given tranquillizers to help her sleep and ease the pain to come.

People suffering from posttraumatic stress disorder also can experience dissociative symptoms when formerly suppressed events are re-experienced in flashbacks, nightmares, and emotional flooding in response to a trigger. The brain seems to have a protective way of suppressing memories or information the person is not emotionally ready to address and gradually allowing bits and pieces to rise to the surface, indicating, at times, an increased readiness to tackle sometimes horrifying events. As therapists, many of us have learned that the best course of treatment may be to gently encourage the uncovering process and provide safeguards should the flooding of unwanted memories occur. Brief hospitalizations for safety are sometimes required. Some patients learn techniques for putting unwanted memories safely in storage until they are ready to "open the door" once again.

The ability to dissociate is a survival skill, but eventually it may prevent a full and rich life. It can also, paradoxically, open the person to additional danger by blocking red flags that would normally arouse concern. For example, a patient I saw many years ago revealed to me that she had been molested for many years by her father, a prominent educator. She had gone on to have two sons of her own and reported allowing her father to babysit for her sons on a regular basis. It was as though the two events had no connection. She also habitually put herself in harm's way without being able to look at her behavior and predict consequences and protect herself. These are examples of a learned dissociative defense not protecting, but endangering the traumatized person.

Hearing voices (auditory hallucinations) are positive symptoms of a schizophrenic disorder, but this may also occur during a psychotic episode in patients with bipolar disorder or psychotic depression. Patients who have experienced severe trauma (especially sexual abuse in childhood) may develop "voices" as well. They can range from replaying of negative and pejorative statements and accusations, to commands to hurt themselves or others, or hearing conversations among the various parts of the personality in dissociative identity disorder.

---

24   American Psychiatric Association, *Desk Reference to the Diagnostic Criteria from the DSM-5*, Washington, DC: American Psychiatric Publishing: 2013, 155-157.

In Great Britain, less emphasis seems to be made on diagnosing the etiology of the voices, and more on providing support and tools to help manage them. In a New York Times series on mental health issues (*Lives Restored: Profiles of Mental Illness*, on August 6, 2011), Benedict Cary interviewed Rufus May, a clinical psychologist, who also experiences auditory hallucinations. Useful techniques were discussed as well as the help of the "Hearing Voices Network"—self-help groups and workbooks. The article can be accessed on the internet under "Changing the Power Relationship with Your Voices."

Antidepressant medications, antianxiety medications, sleep aids, and occasionally mood stabilizers may be prescribed to help the dissociative patient's distressing symptoms. Individual and group therapy in a safe environment are keys to addressing the underlying trauma and improving relationships in the patient's life.

Resources:

Cary, Benedict. "Learning to Cope with a Mind's Taunting Voices". *The New York Times*". August 6, 2011.

Cooper, Terry D. *Accepting the Troll Underneath the Bridge: Overcoming Our Self-Doubts.* Eugene: Wipf & Stock Pub., 2010.

Goulding, Regina A., and Schwartz, Richard C . *The Mosaic Mind: Empowering the Tormented Selves of Child Abuse Survivors.* New York: W.W. Norton & Co.,1995.

Herman, Judith Lewis. *Trauma and Recovery.* New York: BasicBooks, 1997.

Quinn, Phil E. *From Victim to Victory: Prescriptions from a Child Abuse Survivor.* Nashville: Abingdon Press, 1994.

Terr, Lenore. *Unchained Memories: True Stories of Traumatic Memories, Lost and Found.* New York: Basic Books, 1994.

Chapter 33
Dissociative Disorder:
The Eyes Are the Mirror of the Soul

Helene

FOR CENTURIES THE expression "the eyes are the mirror of (or window to) the soul" has been used. Various derivations are given: an old English proverb, and the Bible itself. The *Book of Matthew*, Chapter 6, verses 22-23 says, "The eye is the lamp of the body. So if your eye is healthy, your whole body will be filled with light; but if your eye is unhealthy, your whole body will be filled with darkness." (New Revised Standard Version)

When I was growing up, my Hungarian-American mother used the expression frequently, most often when she distrusted someone. I associated the phrase with pictures of the crazed Charles Manson, to me the epitome of evil.

In my work with trauma survivors I have learned to "read" eyes. The sadness I see there can be profound, and also the frightening rage that pours from the eyes. Years ago, when I was a nursing student, I heard that children with cleft palates often have incredibly beautiful and expressive eyes. I feel the same can be said of many trauma survivors. A particular childlike innocence often radiates from their gaze that gives me a clue to their history. Trauma survivors' eyes can shift as they enter the domain of painful memories and slip into dissociative experiences. At times these people may appear and respond differently than their normal personas. I've caught on to an upward gaze or distraction that may indicate the person is hearing voices, which is common for trauma survivors.

Margaret is the patient I've worked with who best exemplifies eyes being mirrors. We've known each other for close to 15 years. When we first met, Margaret was recently discharged from an adult psychiatric unit following suicidal behavior. She was in an unhappy marriage and dealing with unresolved childhood trauma. Margaret is a beautiful young woman with a glowing complexion, stylishly cropped blond hair, and large violet eyes that would make Elizabeth Taylor jealous. Early on, her personality was subdued and depressed. We focused on her trauma history, especially an abusive grandmother who terrorized her as a small child. She told horrifying tales of being locked in a pitch dark basement. Her grandmother's voice, though subdued and in spite of her death, is periodically still with Margaret today. When Margaret is questioning herself or in an unhealthy relationship, the grandmother's voice returns to criticize and abuse her.

Despite Margaret's abuse and psychiatric history, she is a true survivor. She made numerous devoted friends, finished her advanced education, and has held demanding jobs. Her medical health has been an enormous challenge. Surviving leukemia after a bone marrow transplant over ten years ago is a miracle. Recently, she suffered a health set back that forced her to quit her job. Living with her parents for several years has given her more financial security, but is fraught with conflict and ambivalence.

While convalescing, she brought her father in to one of our meetings. She clearly was having significant medical difficulties and seemed emotionally regressed. Her voice was quiet and childlike, with simple sentence structure. She looked around the room for reassurance and familiarity. (Trauma survivors get comfort from an environment that does not change.) Most indicative of her distress were her eyes. When Margaret is happy, her beautiful violet eyes seem more pronounced, almost protruding from her face. The color is clear and bright, often with a merry twinkle. But when Margaret is under stress, feeling unsure, or, most particularly, when she begins to hear her grandmother's voice, her eyes become dark, the blue-gray of the ocean before a dangerous storm. They seem sunken and lifeless.

My next meeting with Margaret was a great relief. She had made changes at home that made living with her parents less stressful. She'd begun planning for the future and was reconnecting with her good friends. And, most importantly, her eyes were sparkling and enormous, reflecting returned confidence and hope.

My work with Margaret has taught me to be ever mindful and observant of people's expressions, particularly their eyes. I continue to be grateful for this access to the core of a person's being and the privilege of helping with the healing of old wounds.

Chapter 34
Do I Have Bipolar Disorder?

Helene

EACH YEAR MORE people than ever enter our offices with the question "Do you think I'm bipolar?" Increased media awareness of the disorder may be the reason, but even with new public awareness many people live with undiagnosed bipolar disorder for many years. In a recent lecture, Dr. Leslie Citrome reported that up to two thirds of patients with bipolar depression are misdiagnosed. These misdiagnosed patients not only don't receive the treatment they need to recover; they may also receive antidepressant medication that can tip them from depression into hyperactivity and mania.

Before we used the term bipolar disorder, manic depressive illness was used to identify a mood disorder characterized by mood swings ranging from psychotic delusional frenzy to soul crushing suicidal depression. Only a small percentage of people have these extremes, but many more live on what is called the bipolar spectrum, with attributes of the illness, but not full blown dramatic swings.

Certain personality disorders, such as borderline personality disorder, can cause dramatic mood fluctuations as well. Crossover symptoms may also occur between bipolar disorder and attention deficit hyperactivity disorder (e.g., both can lead to racing thoughts and poor concentration). Complicating matters even more is the possibility of comorbidity; that is, having more than one disorder at the same time.

Years ago in my clinical work, I discovered that some patients who suffer from depression do not do well on any stand-alone antidepressant. Even more disturbing is the occasional patient who becomes more depressed, agitated, aggressive, and at times suicidal on antidepressants, displaying symptoms we call hypomanic. Adding a mood stabilizer to the antidepressant often gives nearly immediate relief from these acute symptoms. The recent proliferation of commercials describing a patient who isn't getting better on antidepressants alone has increased public awareness of these mood stabilizing medications, which can literally be lifesavers.

Some patients live their lives more on the manic end of the bipolar spectrum. My patient of over fifteen years, Donna, was one of those. She was referred to me by her primary care physician (PCP) who worried about her lack of improvement and behavior that put her at risk. Donna had a fairly classic manic presentation. She had a larger than life personality with a broad smile, infectious laugh, and pressured, rapid speech. Her humor could be quite colorful. Her mood would quickly switch from joviality to irritability and anger toward people or situations in her life. She was working as a school bus driver which aggravated severe arthritis in her shoulders, hips, and knees, giving her constant, excruciating bone on bone pain. She was constantly worried about finances, which prevented her from taking time off to take care of herself. She couldn't afford to visit her son and his family in California, and that made her sad.

Contrasting with the hypomanic presentation was the depression Donna struggled to hide. She was uncomfortable talking about or displaying her profound sadness. As a result, she concealed it in sessions with me and would isolate with her cats in her apartment, sometimes not coming out for days. Most concerning was her refusal to pick up the phone when she was in a dark mood. She would leave messages indicating that she was in a bad way and then be unreachable. The poem printed at the end of this chapter was written by Donna when she was in a profound depression, before treatment. The poem portrays the deep level of loneliness and hopelessness she felt when she sank into depression.

Earlier in Donna's life, she drank and used drugs to "party" and avoid emotional pain. At times she resorted to cutting behavior to relieve the internal pain. She took risks in relationships and was mistreated by many men. Her level of despair reflected a traumatic childhood, a common theme in the history of adults with chaotic, self-destructive lives.

I've always known that bipolar patients are among my favorite people to treat. For one thing, when the correct medications are finally prescribed, the improvement in their lives can be amazing and satisfying. I also have my own Helene's Litmus Test for diagnosing patients with bipolar disorder. These entertaining folks bring out my own hypomanic side. I find myself laughing and joking within the first session and quickly feel an emotional connection. Bipolar patients often have above average intelligence and are entertaining. But here is the caution: being entertaining can defend against the pain behind the humor and often creates a huge obstacle to doing the painful work in psychotherapy. I have to pull back and refocus the conversation when I sense I'm entertained.

Over the years I've wondered what it would be like to treat patients like Robin Williams or Robert Downy Jr.—charismatic people who have the art of diversion down to a science. It would be so easy to sit back and relax, laugh, and not focus on all the pain behind the eyes. Sadly, depressed bipolar patients have a high risk for suicidal behavior, so those of us who take on the challenging work of treating them are also at risk for a devastating and sometimes unexpected blow when they successfully suicide.

Donna had not been successfully treated with medication before our work together. After a few tries we found a combination of medications that gave her some relief. In her typical humorous way she took to calling me "The Great Oz" because of the difference in her life after the medications, saying I performed magic. She continues to receive psychotherapy from another clinician as well. If I am "The Great Oz," she is David for battling her own personal Goliath and winning.

What is the Bipolar Spectrum?

The bipolar spectrum refers to the psychiatric disorders that are characterized by severe mood fluctuations. Bipolar I disorder has distinct episodes of mania (over-activity) that can involve psychosis and severe depression. "It appears to be caused by a dysregulation in brain chemistry, which can be accentuated by genetics and environmental factors.[25]"

These patients can be at high risk for suicide. Bipolar II disorder also includes fluctuating moods, but the mania is characterized as hypomania and is less extreme than the manic episodes of Type I. The depressions are pronounced and often are the symptom that leads to treatment. Often hypomania is displayed in irritable and aggressive behavior. There are also mood fluctuations observed in substance abusing patients, in ADHD, anxiety disorders, dissociative disorders, psychotic disorders such as schizoaffective disorders, and in personality disorders (particularly borderline personality disorder).

As confusing as the diagnostic picture sounds, careful history gathering with family corroboration, family history to identify genetic predisposition, a history of suicide attempts, early onset of illness, seasonal patterns, and recent childbirth can help identify patients with a bipolar diagnosis. It is reassuring to know that the symptoms of over-activity and depression respond to the same medications regardless of diagnosis.

The careful use of antidepressants, along with prescribed mood stabilizers, is essential to avoid the exacerbation of manic symptoms. Patients with bipolar disorder need to get adequate sleep, because insomnia is a predominant symptom of bipolar and some unipolar depression. Insomnia can be a red flag indicting a worsening of the illness and may also be a destabilizer. After childbirth, mothers

---

25   Suppes, Trisha and Dennehy, Ellen B. , *Bipolar Disorder: The latest assessment and treatment strategies* (Kansas City: Compact Clinicals, 2005), 8.

with bipolar illness or postpartum depression need to be encouraged to get plenty of rest. Family should be enlisted to help with night feedings. The importance of sleep cannot be overemphasized.

It is felt that untreated or inadequately controlled bipolar disorder damages structures of the brain and the medications can be neuro-protective, so rapid assessment and treatment as well as patient compliance will lead to a more positive outcome and fulfilling life. Treating bipolar disorder is a shared process with patient, provider, and family.

What are Mood Stabilizers?

Mood stabilizers are medications that treat and help prevent mood fluctuations. The first mood stabilizer used was lithium, which is still used largely for Bipolar I, manic and mixed (having both the features of mania and depression concurrently). Lithium is generally well tolerated, but needs to be carefully monitored with regular blood levels drawn to avoid serious side effects. Patients taking lithium must stay well hydrated to avoid toxicity that could damage the kidneys. To read about bipolar disorder, its treatment, and how lithium saved a life, read Kay Redfield Jamison's autobiography, *The Unquiet Mind.*[26]

Anticonvulsants such as carbamazepine, lamotrigine, oxcarbazepine, and valproate can be effective in treating bipolar disorder. All require close monitoring, some with periodic blood tests, and have the possibility for side effects such as weight gain, tremors, and sedation. At this point, the prescriber's preference and the patient's response usually determine which medicine is best.

In recent years some prescribers have come to rely on the class of medications known as atypical antipsychotics or second generation antipsychotics to treat our patients with mood fluctuations. These medications including abilify, olanzapine, quetiapine, risperidone, ziprasidone and one of the newest, latuda, are generally well tolerated, require screening blood tests (but not frequent blood levels), and seem to offer antidepressant effects without as much worry of inducing mania as the antidepressant medications. This class of medications may cause metabolic side effects, affecting weight, waist measurement, lipids, and blood glucose. Careful monitoring to prevent complications such as elevated lipids or type 2 diabetes is essential.

---

26   Redfield, Jamison, *The Unquiet Mind: A Memoir of Moods and Madness* (italics), Vintage, 1996.

Into the Winds

A cry called out, carried *into the winds*
How far will I be carried?
For how long will I remain strong before I start to weaken,
be taken from my long journey?
Who will Feed me and give me strength?
I know not where I'm heading.
Will anyone stop for a moment,
on this cold, dark, and windy night to listen?
Will they know I am not a mere whisper
just passing through the naked branches of lonely trees?
But truly a cry for help being tossed out into the winds?
Can anyone hear me?
Tell me I am not alone.

—by DMS, 1984

Resources:

Depression Bipolar Alliance –www.dbsalliance.org

Mood Disorder Questionnaire found in Hirschfeld, RM et al. American Journal of Psychiatry. 2000; 157(11):1873-1875 and www.dbsalliance.org/pdfs/MDQ. pdf.

National Institute of Mental Health—www.nimh.nih.gov

The Unquiet Mind: A Memoir of Mood and Madness by Kay Redfield Jamison (New York: Alfred A. Knopf, 1995)

Chapter 35
Dealing with Adult Attention Deficit Disorder: My Husband Puts Me Down
Helene

JEN SEEMED DEPRESSED when she first entered my office close to 15 years ago, and that was exactly why her gynecologist referred her. She sat with her shoulders slumped and kept her gaze downward, avoiding eye contact. About halfway through the first appointment she asked if I had treated people with ADHD. She'd been reading a book named *Women with Attention Deficit Disorder*[27] by Sari Solden. As she read the book, which a friend had recommended, Jen identified with almost all the symptoms. What disturbed her most was her disorganization, which affected her family life and caused Bill, her highly organized executive husband, to lose patience with her. She was constantly misplacing things, forgetting important appointments, and had trouble managing the house. These difficulties mirror her symptoms while growing up and struggling with school. I could imagine people teasing Jen and calling her "space cadet," then enjoying the reaction on her animated, impish, and responsive face which flushes easily.

Jen concealed her depression with smiles and people-pleasing behaviors. Bill had a stressful career and she did not wish to burden him. Often he came home already exasperated by a work issue and she didn't want her difficulties to further aggravate him, which would cause his irritability to be directed toward her.

Initially I started her on Prozac (fluoxetine) to help with her sadness and sensitivity. Women, especially when premenstrual, often suffer from rejection sensitivity and have a strong negative response to any perceived criticism or

27   Solden, Sari. *Women with Attention Deficit Disorder: Embrace your Differences and Transform your Life*. Nevada City: Underwood Books, 2005.

disrespect. I have found that Prozac and other SSRI antidepressants can help modulate these strong negative responses that are not only damaging to the individual, but to relationships as well. While the Prozac was helpful it did not address the ADHD symptoms that were eroding her self-esteem.

Adderall, a stimulant indicated for ADHD, was our first choice, mainly because I had another adult woman patient with ADHD who benefitted from it. If Jen's children or siblings were successfully treated for ADHD with another medication we would have tried that first, because of genetic similarities. Jen felt more clearheaded almost immediately on the Adderall. She was able to complete tasks with less distraction and frustration.

Jen's symptoms of depression were largely controlled by daily fluoxetine. Occasionally she took trazodone (a sedating antidepressant) to sleep. Ever since Adderall was prescribed for her, she has felt more in control of her life.

Although medication helped Jen feel better, I felt she had problems we needed to discuss in therapy. People with histories of ADHD often have self-esteem issues because of ridicule and bullying at school, from friends, and from family members. When Jen's husband showed annoyance at her disorganization and trouble staying on task or completing projects, hurt feelings from her childhood would emerge and worsen her depression or cause her to defend herself, which led to arguments.

After starting the medication Jen had been avoiding discussing old hurts and tended to focus on current life issues, which were abundant. She did a fabulous job managing her household while planning and arranging several moves, supporting two talented preteen and teenaged children and sending them to college, being active in school functions, working part-time and pursuing her artistic talents. Her athlete children both suffered complex injuries that required patience and self-education on her part. Jen was able to comfort and support and care for them through many emergencies. This self-described "airhead" mastered the science of traumatic brain injuries and orthopedic care. Her husband and children benefitted from and appreciated her ability to focus on medical complications that would have caused many parents to panic and run.

More recently, in my office, Jen looked youthful, energetic, and attractive. Her blond bouncy curls were barely contained by a scrungee and, once again, she was straight from the shower with a wet head, running late for her early morning appointment. She will face new challenges as her children mature and her husband retires, but her story is a wonderful example how women with ADHD can lead satisfying and productive lives. Jen's delightful impulsivity and humor have remained and will always be part of who she is. I thank Jen for educating me about women with ADHD and giving me an example I have shared with many people.

What is ADHD?

Attention deficit hyperactivity disorder is a condition that affects the entire life span, is generally present before age 12, and has a genetic component. Symptoms identified in the *DSM-5* (Diagnostic Manual of the American Psychiatric Association) are the following: inattention: carelessness, difficulty remaining focused, not seeming to listen, difficulty staying on task, disorganization, avoidance of complex tasks, losing possessions, being easily distracted, and forgetful; hyperactivity and impulsivity: fidgety, trouble staying seated, restless, noisy, talking excessively, cannot wait turn, interrupting others.

It's important to treat ADHD when it is causing social, educational and emotional distress, because patients with untreated ADHD have a significantly higher percentage of substance abuse, violent criminal activity, and may also develop depression and bipolar disorders. Patients can be coached regarding behavioral techniques to enhance organization and memory (phone reminders, post-its, prominent calendars, etc.) but may require medication to lead the productive lives they wish to have.

What Medications Help Adult ADHD?

The same medications used to treat children with ADHD can be effective in adults. In fact, it isn't uncommon for parents of treated children to recognize the symptoms in themselves and request the same medications that helped their children. The genetic component of the disorder supports that plan of action. As in other disorders, such as depression and bipolar disorder, the first medication tried is often one that was effective for a blood relative.

"The most commonly used agents to enhance attention in attention deficit disorder are the stimulants methylphenidate and d-amphetamine. Both of these medications increase available dopamine in the brain."[28]

Stimulants tend to have calming effects and increase mental focus in patients with ADHD. Medications that increase norepinephrine in the brain may be effective for some patients with ADD. Bupropion and amoxapine may be good first choices, especially if there is concern about the potential for medication misuse or abuse. Possible misuse of the medications may be cause for concern when prescribing to at-risk populations (young adults, and patients with criminal records or histories of medication misuse). Longer acting stimulants such as Adderall XR and Vyvanse may be less susceptible to diversion and misuse than the shorter acting versions that may be crushed and snorted.

---

28 Stahl, Stephen M., *Essential Psychopharmacology* (Cambridge, UK: Cambridge University Press, 2000) 461.

Resources:

Adult ADHD Self-Report Scales (ASRS), HTTP://www. hcp.med.harvard.edu/ncs/asrs.

Hallowell, Edward M. and Ratey, John J. *Driven to Distraction: Recognizing and Coping with Attention Deficit Disorder.* New York: Anchor, 2011.

Kelly, Kate and Ramundo, Peggy. *You Mean I'm Not Lazy, Stupid or Crazy.* New York: Scribner, 2006.

Solden, Sari. *Women with Attention Deficit Disorder: Embrace your Differences and Transform your Life.* Nevada City: Underwood Books, 2005.

Chapter 36
Cancer Diagnosis: It's All In Your Head
Patricia

ONE DAY A FIT looking woman who appeared around sixty years of age entered my therapy office and said, "Dr. Martin, you're my last hope. I've seen several doctors to no avail and I still feel nauseous on a daily basis. All the doctors tell me they can't find any physical problem. They think it's all in my head and suggested I see you."

Although Jane had never before had psychotherapy, she was willing to try it because she was "darned tired of feeling sick." She and her retired physician husband had just moved to the area from the west coast to be near her daughter and grandchildren. She was ready and eager to enjoy retirement, but every day brought another round of vomiting. Now, she wanted to make sure this wasn't all in her head.

I conducted six or seven sessions with Jane, gently probing to determine from a thorough personal history if she had unresolved issues that might cause the vomiting.

Sometimes when someone begins recalling childhood sexual abuse they experience waves of nausea. However, in Jane's case I didn't detect any abuse. I also explored possible unresolved issues surrounding her recent move to the area, but again come up empty. She and her husband were thrilled to retire and eager to get on with the joys of grand-parenting and recreational living. I did a thorough family psychiatric history, but in the end I found Jane was fine psychologically; except for her despair at not knowing why the vomiting was happening.

She then awaited a visit with a gastroenterologist who specialized in cyclic vomiting syndrome. After seeing the gastroenterologist, Jane learned she had abdominal migraines, started on medication, and began feeling better. We decided she no longer needed to see me for psychotherapy and should begin enjoying her retirement.

She was happy, back on track, and said she'd call me in the future if needed. Six months passed with no word from Jane. As I often do, I thought about her and wondered how she was doing. One day while I was pondering Jane's life I received a call from her husband who wanted to visit and update me on all that had transpired since Jane's last visit six months earlier.

Her husband Jack was a soft spoken, deliberate, rational man who'd never before entered a therapy office. He wanted me to know what happened to Jane because she enjoyed our therapy and he thought I'd want to know. I assured him I was very interested and had just been thinking of Jane the week he called.

Jack looked tired and worn out the day he came to see me. His eyes teared up as he spoke about his dear wife. He explained that Jane became dizzy about a month after being diagnosed with stomach migraines. She went to a neurologist who said she had vertigo, but he wanted to run a routine MRI before prescribing medication. Thankfully, the MRI spotted something they had overlooked up to that point. Jane had a brain tumor; a medulloblastoma. The tumor was wrapped around her cerebellum and she required immediate surgery.

Jane underwent surgery and survived, but had complications and was hospitalized for two months after surgery. Then she caught pneumonia. She was treated, recovered from the pneumonia, and spent two months in rehabilitation to learn to talk, swallow, walk, and care for herself. She was able to go home for two months, only to return to the hospital with an infection. The infection was treated and she had been home for a month and a half.

After describing in detail what Jane went through, Jack stopped and looked at me. We looked eye to eye for about ten seconds and then he began to cry. He cried a few minutes and then gathered himself together and whispered, "We almost lost her."

He wanted to see me for support because I knew, loved, and appreciated Jane as a wonderful woman. Jack felt distraught, confused, and afraid of losing her. He wondered if he would ever get back the "old Jane," even if she survived.

I tried to reassure him, telling him what a wonderful advocate he was being for his wife and pointing out she needed him now more than ever. I counseled Jack for the next two months to help him process all the things he and Jane had gone through. He told me Jane was eager to see me again. She was eight months post surgery; she could talk, was eating, and able to walk, although having balance issues. She had double vision, but was no longer vomiting. Jane spoke highly of all the doctors and nurses who helped her and cared for her along the way. She wanted to see me and worked hard with her physical therapy so she could get to my office.

Jack and I scheduled an appointment for the next week. He would drive Jane, but she wanted to meet with me alone. I prepared myself before Jane's visit by trying to visualize what she might look like. I knew she lost weight and had trouble talking and walking. I also imagined the double vision might impair her ability to have direct eye contact.

She entered my office and immediately chirped in her new little voice, "It's so good to see you, Dr. Martin! I'm so glad to be alive and I want to tell you all that happened since I last saw you."

I told her I could hardly wait to hear about all she'd gone through during the past six months.

Jane told me she remembered nothing of her two month stay in the hospital, when she was in the intensive care unit in a psychotic state, pulling out her tracheal tube and dressings. She had no memory of this, but did remember writing a letter to her two children before surgery. The letter was to be shredded if she survived. She told me Jack had torn it up a few weeks earlier. Jane spoke of how lucky she was to have such a loving, devoted husband. Jack got her the best surgeons and made all her follow up appointments. He stayed at her bedside every day for three and a half months while she was in and out of the hospital. Jane wanted me to know how grateful she was that I could see Jack and give him support while she was in rehabilitation. He had never been to a "shrink" before and he liked me.

Jane said she felt she'd finally made it and was on the road to recovery. Today was her twenty-ninth day of radiation with one more day to go. Her hair was ragged and falling out, but she wore the biggest smile. Her voice was squeaky, but it would get better. She was seeing an ophthalmologist the next day for her double vision.

She told me her biggest upset was when she thought she might never eat again because of the inability to swallow. At that point she didn't want to live anymore, but knew she wouldn't kill herself. She just wanted to eat again. And she could, except steak and rolls. She said, "I can live just fine without them."

Jane added, "Now I want to travel." She and Jack were planning a trip to Michigan to Mackinac Island. She also had a goal of riding a bike again with Jack, who is an avid cycler. I told her she has made amazing progress and I am sure she will continue to do well.

She especially wanted to tell me how much she appreciated the fact that I didn't tell her the vomiting was "all in her head." She laughed and said, "But I guess it really was all in my head," referring to the brain tumor.

We laughed together, I gave her a big hug, and let her know I would be here if she ever needed me. She smiled, said, "I'll let you know," and walked out my office door. I told myself, "What a wonderful, brave woman she is." I am grateful for meeting Jane and her devoted husband, and I sometimes reflect on how much they taught me about gratitude, love, and persistence.

Patricia Peters Martin, Ph.D.
Helene DeMontreux Houston, M.S., APRN

Resources:

www.mayoclinic.org/diseases

www.abta.org (American Brain Tumor Association)

Cyclic vomiting syndrome: Cyclic vomiting syndrome is characterized by episodes of severe vomiting that have no apparent cause. Episodes can last for hours or days and alternate with relatively symptom-free periods of time. Each episode is similar to previous ones, meaning that episodes tend to start at the same time of day, last the same length of time and occur with the same symptoms and level of intensity. Cyclic vomiting syndrome occurs in all age groups. It may be related to migraines.

Abdominal Migraines: An abdominal migraine is a variant of a migraine headache, but the pain occurs in the belly. In theory, abdominal migraines are caused by changes in two chemicals, histamine and serotonin. Daily stress and anxiety can cause fluctuations in these body chemicals. Abdominal migraines are rare in adults, but about 2% of children are diagnosed with them. The symptoms are acute, severe, midline abdominal pain that is associated with nausea, vomiting, paleness, and an inability to eat.

Brain Tumors of the Cerebellum: Medulloblastoma is a fast-growing, high-grade tumor always located in the cerebellum, the lower, rear portion of the brain. The most common symptoms of medulloblastoma include behavioral changes, changes in appetite, symptoms of increased nausea, vomiting, and drowsiness, as well as problems with coordination. Unusual eye movements may also occur. Treatment consists of surgical removal of as much tumor as possible, radiation, and then chemotherapy.

Chapter 37
Chronic Suicidal Ideation: The Bottle of Aspirin
Helene

SUICIDAL THINKING, combined with a well-thought-out plan and intent is one of the most challenging and terrifying symptoms a client can reveal in therapy. As therapists we walk a tightrope, balancing the client's safety with maintaining privacy and the therapeutic alliance. Fortunately, most clients do not act on their thoughts, but the danger is real.

I met thirty-seven-year-old Ruth fifteen years ago after her discharge from a psychiatric unit where she was admitted for suicidal ideation. Ruth was a short, blond woman with gray blue eyes that would alternately drift off or look at me with pleading intensity. Eventually that look would be accompanied by the question, "Am I ever going to get better?"

Ruth's palpable sadness came from a childhood filled with sexual abuse, a bipolar and unstable husband, and a sexual attack as an adult, leaving her with unremitting suicidal depression. She felt hopeless and wished to end her pain. When we began treatment her younger son Jeremy was fifteen. She announced firmly and often "When Jeremy is eighteen, I'm going to kill myself."

Ruth told me she began wishing and planning for her death as a small child. The sexual abuse was ongoing and she recalled at age four, pulling a stool up to the bathroom sink every day to see if the aspirin was still there. The sight of the aspirin bottle soothed her because somehow she knew ingesting it could end her emotional pain.

Jeremy's eighteenth birthday came and went. Ruth had benefitted from a dialectical behavior therapy (DBT) group that had helped distract her from suicidal thoughts and replace them with more positive images. For a time, wearing a necklace that had belonged to a beloved and loving grandmother was her soothing behavior. She planted a garden that gave her pleasure and distraction as a memorial to the grandmother. Unfortunately, Ruth periodically went through emotional crises over which she had no control. On one occasion she punished herself by intentionally exposing herself to poison ivy. The severe allergic reaction resulted in a medical and then psychiatric admission. Mood stabilizers as well as her DBT skills helped her refocus.

Ruth's life was enriched by the marriages of her older son and daughter and the grandchildren who followed. She was available to the families as they dealt with crises of their own, often supplying childcare and lots of love.

Much of Ruth's identity and self-esteem were connected to her work as a health care professional, but an adverse reaction to medication affected her memory and resulted in her dismissal. We'd been working together for many years at that time, but I still worried this incident would bring back her suicidal behavior. After a few rough months that required extra support and more intensive treatment, we spoke of her suicidal ideation and what had become of it.

"How were you able to get through losing your job without feeling suicidal?" I asked.

"I thought of my grandchildren," she said with a big smile.

For soothing herself, Ruth no longer fixated on the bottle of aspirin or thoughts of ending her pain; she thought of the wonderful grandchildren who brought her great joy and love. She had *become* the soothing grandmother and it made her life essential. Her family needed her, and she needed them.

When Ruth learned I wished to write a chapter about her experiences with chronic suicidality and recovery, she asked to share important words of wisdom that may help others who share a similar story, and inspire the therapists who struggle to help and keep them alive.

Ruth's Wisdom

Most patients who commit suicide are not "selfish bastards" who don't care about the pain they leave behind. They have lost all hope and cannot see beyond the hopelessness.

Who are Chronically Suicidal People?

Patients who attempt suicide unsuccessfully or live with chronic suicidal ideation are not being dramatic or seeking attention. They are desperately looking for a glimmer of hope that will keep them alive one day more.

Words of Wisdom for the Therapist, Born from Experience:

- Remember that the option of suicide is a strong tool for staying alive. It provided me comfort that no matter what I endured or how badly I felt, there was a way out.

- I did not see death as romantic, or as revenge to get back at people. As a child, I saw it beyond my age level, as an end to pain and hurt. I knew it was final; we do not come back.
- Know what you are doing. Do not run from the suicidal patient. Listen, learn, ask the right questions and, when possible, contract for safety. When necessary, hospitalize for the patient's safety, not because the patient is "too hot to handle."
- Have a plan for the patient. If he or she cannot contract for safety, know in advance what options are available. If this is not your area of expertise, get help, but do not abandon a suicidal patient.
- Do not pull away the comfort tool of suicide until you replace it with survival tools that have been taught, learned, and have become part of the patient. What got me through was faith, remembered love from grandparents, loving grandchildren and family, and two great therapists who gave me the tools I needed to live. Medication and my willingness to do the work were essential.

Ruth's Goals for the Suicidal Trauma Survivor:

- You are not in this alone, although it feels that way.
- HOPE IS REAL. It is possible to move from victim to survivor and from survival to RECOVERY. It isn't easy, but recovery is wonderful!

Statistics and assessment of risk for patients with chronic suicidal ideations:

The National Institute of Mental Health via its website (nimh.nih.gov) shares the following statistics:

Each year in the United States there are approximately 40,000 deaths due to suicide.

Men are more likely to die of suicide attempts (often by lethal means such as guns or hanging), while women are more likely to attempt suicide—most often by overdoses and poison.

Suicide is the second leading cause of death in the fifteen to twenty-four year old age group.

White males age eighty-five and older have the highest suicide rate.

Screening tools have been developed to identify people who are at risk for depression and suicidal behavior. Columbia University has pioneered the Columbia Suicide Severity Rating Scale (www.cssrs.columbia.edu) to incorporate suicide risks. This scale is a valuable tool to identify patients most at risk for suicide attempts.

What is dialectical behavior therapy?

This treatment is a form of cognitive behavioral therapy developed by Marsha Linehan, Ph.D. in the 1970s to help treat patients with chronically suicidal behavior who shared the characteristics of those with borderline personality disorder (instability and impulsivity, recurrent self-harm, including suicidal behavior). The therapy involves group work for teaching skills that help patients manage impulses to self-harm. Grounding and mindfulness techniques are used. This treatment is especially effective for patients with a history of severe abuse and PTSD.

The patients use workbooks and have individual therapists as well. Mindfulness concepts are a central focus of the therapy.

What medications are used to treat depression?

Until the late 1980s when fluoxetine (Prozac) was introduced, only tricyclic antidepressant medications and MAO inhibitors were available. Unfortunately, those medications burdened patients with numerous side effects. Additionally, tricyclics are severely cardiotoxic and they and MAO inhibitors can be lethal in overdose. The newer class of medication, SSRIs (selective serotonin reuptake inhibitors), is much safer, but can have problems with side effects such as weight gain, sexual dysfunction, and occasionally precipitating agitation or acute onset of suicidal ideation. Other, newer antidepressants are available that work on different combinations of neurotransmitter receptor sites (norepinephrine, dopamine). Occasionally the response to antidepressants is not as robust as one would want, so they may be augmented by a mood stabilizer.

Final Words

Chapter 38
Poverty:
It's Hard to be Compliant When You're Hungry
Helene

AT TIMES I FIND it difficult to settle down and focus on women's wisdom after a week of working with patients who have severe psychiatric illness superimposed on survival issues.

How does one counsel improved judgment and medication compliance when the young woman patient is contemplating living in her car? How can a brittle diabetic in a violent marriage discuss her mood swings when she finds the Open Pantry emptied of the food she needs for her six children, and she can't afford lifesaving fresh fruits and vegetables?

Developing wisdom calls for particular personality qualities and clear thinking. Physical illness, fear, and hunger all interfere with the thinking process. So unless people's basic needs are met, it's unlikely that mature wisdom will develop. Desperation has that effect.

People in these circumstances need a hand up. Home and Community Based Support Services (HCBS) provide government assistance to a variety of targeted groups, and this is one way our society lends a hand. However, if a patient is awarded disability benefits (SSI), which may add Medicare to the mix, that person is no longer eligible for HCBS. Since it's difficult to be certified as eligible for disability benefits, isn't this the population that most needs these supportive services?

If our society even hopes to achieve collective wisdom and enlightenment, we must provide a safety net for the most needy. Not all noncompliant behavior reflects passive aggressive behavior or disrespect. Sometimes patients in these most dire circumstances do not keep their appointments or take their medicine as prescribed. A three dollar copay can be enormous to someone who has no money at all. Bus fare can be prohibitive.

In this tough health care environment, it's easy for clinicians' and doctors' offices to become frustrated and angry with non-compliant patients. Practices are productivity driven and many clinicians work under fee for service, meaning they get paid by the number of patients they can pack into a day's time. That means when a client doesn't show up the clinician won't be paid. This financial concern and worry can be an obstacle to getting to know each patient and compassionately exploring what is interfering with compliance.

Some traditional therapists interpret non-compliance as acting out or resistance to treatment no matter what the circumstances. Sometimes problem solving can resolve the issue. For example, when the patient runs out of money for copays, working on putting money safely aside as soon as the disability check comes in can solve that problem. Helping a patient feel understood and not treated like an irresponsible burden can enhance the therapeutic alliance and compliance. A true win-win for everyone.

Chapter 39
Sage Advice: This One Thing I Know
Patricia

SOME CLIENTS ENTER my office for one session, and though I never see them again, they leave a lasting impression. Such was the case with Helen. I received a call about a week before our session asking to schedule an appointment. When I inquired why she was seeking counseling, with an elderly quiver in her voice she said her internist suggested she come to see me. She chose not to elaborate over the phone and I left it at that.

I was curious about this phone call from the beginning, because the woman on the phone didn't seem eager to see me. When I asked her if she could make it upstairs to my office, she gruffly said, "I'm old, but not an invalid. Of course, I can make stairs."

The next week when she arrived in my waiting room, my suspicions about Helen's lack of desire to be at a psychologist's office were confirmed. She complained when I opened my office door that it was difficult for her to find my office, and "those stairs were a doozy." She left the waiting room chair in a huff and entered my office.

After the preliminary introductions and insurance business were taken care of, I asked Helen what brought her to see me. Again, this elderly, tall, thin woman almost barked at me that her internist told her she should seek counseling. "I only came because my doctor said I was depressed and I needed to talk to someone. I guess that means you." Helen added that she strictly followed her doctor's orders.

I realized at that moment I must proceed gingerly in order to obtain any useful information from this stubborn old coot of a woman.

As I began asking questions about her recent life, Helen relaxed a bit and shared some of her story with me. She had recently lost her last remaining relative, her younger brother. He was eighty-seven and a bachelor who lived in New York City. She went on to tell me he was a writer and they communicated daily. Helen was rather stoic as she related his passing, but said she has not been herself since his death.

When I asked what that meant, she said she cried daily and had lost some of her appetite. I explored further and discovered she was still eating quite well, sleeping alright and was not contemplating suicide. When I asked if she was thinking about hurting herself, she laughed, and said, "At ninety-two years of age I'm not going to knock myself off. I've lived through a lot in my lifetime and this won't put me under."

My jaw dropped to hear she was ninety-two. Helen was definitely the oldest person who'd ever been in my therapy office. I told her I really didn't think she needed therapy and that she was grieving her brother in a normal fashion. She said she didn't think she needed to see me either, but she always followed her doctor's orders, being from "the old school."

I let her know she seemed like a real survivor and she said, "Yep, you're probably right about that."

I asked if she had any secrets of how to survive ninety-two years on this earth. She laughed, looked directly at me, and said "Well, there is one motto I've held onto throughout my adult life." I waited with bated breath for her words:

She went on, *"Expect change, accept change, adapt to change, and don't whine."*

WOW! I told her I thought that was a great way to think and would she mind if I shared her motto with other patients. She grinned at me rather coyly and said, "Sure, do whatever you like with it Dr. Martin. I guess I'm an old dog who can teach some new tricks."

I agreed. When the session ended I walked her to the front door and we exchanged a hug. I sincerely told Helen it was my pleasure meeting her and if she ever needed to see me, just give a holler.

She said, "That won't be necessary, but I did enjoy my time with you."

As she walked to the van that waited to take her back to her assisted living home, I thought of what a valuable lesson I'd just learned from a very wise old woman.

I have shared this adage with several people since my encounter with Helen. One of them was a colleague of mine who was diagnosed with Parkinson's disease. I see this person once a year for meetings at my alma mater where we sit on a board together. At one of the dinners she related how it was becoming more and more difficult to attend the meetings because of her condition. She said she thought this would be her last event.

I asked her if she wanted to hear some advice from a sage client of mine. She was all ears. About a week later I received a text from my friend saying she remembered, "Expect change, accept change and don't whine," but she forgot the fourth part. I immediately responded with the "adapt to change" part and she thanked me. She said these words were helping her adjust to the gradual loss of functioning as her Parkinson's advanced. She also suggested I share these words with more people in my practice because they were words of sage advice and wisdom. And so I share them with the hope of helping you.

Expect change,
accept change,
adapt to change,
and don't whine.

Chapter 40
Finding Inner Peace: A Tag Sale Discovery
Patricia

WHEN KAY ENTERED my office ten years ago she had just broken up with her significant other, with whom she'd been living for five years. The break up left her feeling devastated, alone, and desolate. Her relationship ended in a negative way when she finally told her partner she felt verbally abused and could no longer take the negative energy that was constantly between them. Her partner told her, "Then get out."

Kay had to leave with no place to go. As Kay told her story, I clearly saw she'd been in a negative, verbally abusive partnership. However, it was also apparent that Kay stayed in this relationship for many years because of her insecurity about finances and a need to find a home. Then followed Kay's story, a life story with so many twists and turns it was almost unbelievable to me.

Kay is a short, middle aged woman who carries a few extra pounds around her middle, with a fashion sense like a J Jill model. She has been a Weight Watcher devotee for years, yet enjoys eating and food as much as any foodie I know. She will talk about her dinners out or with her family with such relish and enthusiasm that your mouth waters as she describes her meal. Yet it is only now she can even mention her family, as it took a long time for her to reconnect with them.

This story is the journey of a sixty-six year old woman who spent her life trying to find a home. She began life in a large French Catholic family in Western Massachusetts, the fifth child in a family of eight children. Her father was a laborer who had a serious problem with alcohol and would come home regularly and abuse his wife. If that wasn't enough to quench his anger he would move on to abusing the children. It's no wonder the stress of this life lead to chronic illness and eventual cancer for Kay's mother. She died when Kay was six years of age. Within a year Kay's father committed suicide.

At that point all the children were split up and farmed off to different family members. Kay was sent to an aunt and uncle who did little more than put food on the table. There was no love and affection, nor would there be for many years to come. A family still eluded Kay. When she turned sixteen she sought solace in a convent school and began the preparation for becoming a nun. She thought this would be a loving, nurturing family. Much to her surprise and despair, she found the convent was an environment of emotional deprivation and hostility.

Before making her final vows into the convent life, she asked to speak to a psychologist. Thankfully, Kay discovered this was not the life for her and she left the convent. She began teaching as a lay teacher in the Catholic school system, and not many years later met a nice young man who was the first person she ever dated. She said he was kind to her and she met his family and that sealed the deal. They were married within a year and started building a family right away.

Kay and her husband got along well and had three children within eight years. He held a high paying job as a sales person and they lived a good life together until Kay started working for a jewelry company. She became one of their most successful sales people and attended many conferences for top salesmen. At this conference she met "the love of her life." Until meeting Fran, she'd never let herself admit she was always attracted to women. For the first time in her life she truly felt the warmth of love and true companionship. When she left her husband, their high school aged children rejected their mother and chose to live with their father.

This was in the 1980s, a time that leaving a heterosexual marriage and starting a lesbian relationship was considered deviant, immoral behavior. These women were scorned by society. Kay was devastated by losing her children while trying to be true to herself. Unfortunately, her partner was not as enthralled with Kay, and the relationship only lasted six months.

Kay was now in her early fifties with little job training and no family. She decided to go back to teaching, but she didn't have a teaching license or the credentials to be a certified teacher. She took a low paying job as a para-professional and tried to connect with women in the lesbian community while living in an efficiency apartment and barely paying the bills. Her children were not interested in being in her life because she had devastated their father with her decision to leave him. She was forlorn, but never thought of suicide as she knew in her heart she was being true and honest to herself. She prayed and hoped that someday her life would change and improve.

Within a year she met an older woman who became her partner, and within a few months Kay moved in with Sue. Kay felt that she had "come home." Sue had financial independence from family money. She had a nice house and let Kay decorate and make it a home. But, it wasn't long into the relationship that

Sue began trying to control Kay's every movement. She wouldn't let her go out with friends, she forbade Kay to have any contact with her ex-husband or her children, and she repeatedly put down Kay calling her, stupid, a loser, a leech, and worthless. It took five years for Kay to find the strength and courage to leave this abusive woman.

Often, in verbally abusive relationships the abuser has so whittled down the victim's self-confidence and esteem that they cannot leave the abuser. They begin believing they're worthless and no one will ever love them. After Kay ended the relationship with Sue, she began therapy with me to help her move forward and find a better life.

When I met Kay she was uncertain about her decision to leave Sue. She kept doubting herself and would focus on all the positives of the relationship rather than the abusive behavior. All of this was a moot point, as Sue had told Kay if she left she would never take her back.

But Kay continued to waver about her decision and felt she made a mistake. My job was to reaffirm her choice and let her grieve all the losses she suffered time after time in her life. Now Kay had to find the peace and family she so desperately wanted.

Then at a tag sale she found a box full of tapes—audio tapes from the old fashioned tape players. The tag sale person said no one had been interested in the tapes since people didn't use tape players anymore, so she gave them to Kay. And thus began the journey of Gangaji and Kay's path to enlightenment.

Gangaji is an American born, spiritual teacher and author on natural intelligence. Her book, *The Diamond in Your Pocket*[29] is about discovering your true radiance and inner wisdom. The core message of Gangaji is "always, every instant, every moment, in every circumstance, silent awareness is alive in you." She states on Twitter "Allowing yourself to be as you are is the end of the spiritual search, the end of the path. No ledges, no holds, just free falling."

In another tweet, Gangaji says, "Underneath all the stories, we can experience that deep core of ourselves that is historyless, genderless and parentless."

Kay found listening to her tapes and lectures both relaxing and enlightening. She learned to discover the serenity of letting go of everything: her past, her worries for the future, and to live in the here and now. She learned to accept, "it is what it is." That became her mantra and her means of finding peace in her daily life.

As her therapist I tried to become more educated about Gangaji and her practices. I encourage people to try new approaches, and if something works for them and isn't harming anyone one else, then go for it. Kay gave me one of the tapes to listen to and quite honestly I didn't get it. But it worked for Kay and that's

---

29   Gangaji, *The Diamond in Your Pocket: Discovering Your True Radiance*, Boulder: Sounds True Press, 2007.

what matters to me as her therapist. Whenever Kay starts to worry about the future or fret about the past, she takes out one of her tapes and listens. It works! She becomes more aware of the present moment in all its beauty, and trusts that God will take care of her and help her make future life decisions. She has found serenity and lives day to day, enjoying the beauty of nature all around her and the wonders of discovering newness every day.

During this period of self-discovery, Kay began to reconnect with her three children and ex-husband. Her peacefulness and independence allowed her family to open up to their mother once again. She began sharing holidays with them and helped plan her daughter's wedding. She and her ex became friends and enjoyed a platonic relationship that involved sharing meals with their children and participating as parents of adult children. She was involved in her two sons' lives and enjoyed being a part of a family once again.

A great tragedy befell her during this time when her youngest son, in his thirties, was accidentally shot and killed while in military service. Kay's world was shattered and she fell into doubt, remorse, and anger over the circumstances of his death.

I thought, "Why?" I sometimes reflected on Kay being tested like Job in the Old Testament. I worried she wouldn't manage to recover from this loss. She was angry, sure there was a cover up of the circumstances around her son's death. She pursued legal counsel, but was told it was a losing battle.

Kay had difficulty letting go of the feeling that something bad had been covered up and several years passed before she could truly lay her son to rest in her mind. But the wisdom and words of Gangaji again helped her find the way back. My role was to support her through this grief, helping her regain the strength and will to continue to be part of her family and her world of friendship.

Kay's eternal optimism has helped her throughout all these tragedies in her life. She can now awaken every day with the belief that all will be well. No matter what shakes her world, she has a true inner belief that she will be fine. Her inner peace is seldom shaken now and she continues on her journey of self-discovery.

Resources:
The Diamond in Your Pocket: Discovering Your True Radiance, by Gangaji, Boulder: Sounds True Press, 2007.
www.gangaji.org

Meditation Resources:
www.freemeditation.com
www.freemindfulness.org
www.mindfulnesscds.com

Chapter 41
Are You My Grandma? What's In A Name
Patricia

IF YOU HAVE CHILDREN, you know that naming a child can be complicated. People use books, websites, family lineage, and other resources to help them come up with the perfect names. You walk around with an endless list of first and middle names swirling inside your head. During my time of pregnancy, before we knew the sex of the child we made two lists, one for girls and one for boys. Finding a name both of us liked was a major task, and I found you can learn a lot about your spouse through this process—but that's another story.

Now, for those of us in our fifties and sixties who are fortunate enough to be grandparents, the name game begins again. This time we get to decide what those precious grandchildren will call us. Long gone are the days of Grandma and Grandpa. We live in the age of designer grandparent labels. I've heard Gigi, Dodo, Mimi, Vivi, Memah, Toots, G, Mim, Giggy, Soo Soo, and GG. But, does it really matter what we call ourselves?

As William Shakespeare wrote in Romeo and Juliet, "A rose by any other name still smells as sweet." But in their book *Freakonomics,*[30] Steven Levitt and Stephen Dubner dispute Shakespeare's statement. In the chapter "Perfect Parenting, Part II," the authors provide statistics that show the names you select will affect your child's entire future. Scary thought!

Does this hold true for naming ourselves as grandparents? Will our names have any impact on the relationship with our grandchildren? One of my male friends said he didn't pick a name; he just waited until the grandchildren called

---

30   Levitt, Steven D. and Dubner, Stephen, *Freakonomics: A Rogue Economist Explores the Hidden Side of Everything*, William Morrow, 2009.

him something. Well, I am not sure I want to take that chance. For one friend of mine such an encounter ended with the name "BABUTZ"....ah... no way is MABUTZ going to be my moniker.

When I asked friends about their chosen grandparent name, few of them went with the traditional Grandma and Grandpa. I think this is because those names conjure up images of white haired old women wearing aprons and a feeble grandpa walking with a cane.

When I knew my daughter was expecting, I wrote the list of possible names pulled off the internet, looked up ethnic names, thought about my grandparents' and parents' names (Grammie and Grandmom) and asked people I knew what they called themselves. Being of Lithuanian, Irish, and English descent I searched those ethnic names and came up with Nanny, Nana, and Bobki. My mother went by Grammie in honor of her favorite Grandmother and my grandmothers were both Grandmom. None of these names rang true for me, so I continued searching.

Finally, I decided on a French form of Grandmother, since I studied French in high school and college. MeMe (with an accent aigu on the e's). It worked for me, although it can be hard to pronounce for many. My own mother calls me Mammy when referring to my grandmother name, as she can't remember the MeMe pronunciation. Generally, I break out in a rendition of an Al Jolson tune from *The Jazz Singer* when she calls me that. However my first grandchild, Charlotte, was happy to oblige by calling me MeMe. I think she was able to say it by one year of age and this continued through all my visits to see her throughout her first two and a half years of life. Her paternal grandmother goes by GG.

I went along happily being beckoned in the morning with MeMe and teaching her words in French like "bonjour," "au revoir," and "ooh la la." Charlotte particularly loved to say "les poisson, les poisson" after watching the Little Mermaid movie. And so we lived happily ever after, until a visit to Charlotte when she was nearing three years of age. I generally fly into Washington D.C. for my visits in the morning while my granddaughter is at her morning session of preschool. My daughter had informed the preschool teacher, Miss Judy, that her mom was coming for a visit. So when Miss Judy said to Charlotte, "I understand you have a special visitor coming to see you today; your grandma," Charlotte politely nodded and went on her way to the sand table. When she arrived home from school, Charlotte was excited to see me and ran to my arms. We had our usual love fest with lots of kisses and hugs, and then my sweet grandchild looked me straight in the eyes and asked, "MeMe, are you my Grandma?"

My heart melted and I said "Yes, Charlotte, I am your Grandma." My statement echoed like the editorial in The New York Sun of 1897, "Yes, Virginia, there is a Santa Claus." A look of utter happiness and joy filled my little granddaughter's face and her body was shaking, literally shaking, with delight when she screamed out loud, "YOU are MY Grandma?"

I realized this sweet little child did not think she had a grandma. She knew she had a MeMe and a GG, who loved her very much; but where was Grandma? Even though I'd told her in the past I was her grandmother, it must have been beyond her understanding at that time.

Well, you can imagine how the rest of the visit unfolded. At every turn I was beckoned by the name "GrandMa (accent on the Ma). I felt like I was on the TV show, *The Waltons* or *Little House on the Prairie*. And for an even greater effect, Charlotte began calling me Grandmother. Imagine hearing her little voice at 7 a.m. calling for me to get her from her crib with the words, "Grandmother, Grandmother?" After a couple months the Grandmother nickname was dropped, but now six months later I'm known by a combination of either Grandma or MeMe.

Perhaps after all, Grandma is not such a bad name; and maybe I need to stop dying my hair, and maybe it's time for the return of the bun; and maybe I need to wear more aprons......NAAAHHH, that might be going a bit too far. But Grandma, with the accent on the MA works fine for me!

Next on the agenda for Charlotte may be understanding that Papa Jimbo is really GrandPa.

This Chapter taken in part from article, *Finding Love, not Aging, in Being Called GrandMA,* published in Mass-Live, January 26, 2014

Chapter 42
Random Acts of Kindness: The Angel Lady
Patricia

SOMETIMES WE FIND kindness and compassion in the most unlikely places. I found them in a woman who calls herself The Angel Lady. To many people, this diminutive, aquamarine-blue-eyed, sixty-five-year-old woman with heavy blue eye shadow and bright red hair (you know, the kind of red that screams, "What were you thinking when you made that dye choice?)" is considered a bit eccentric. She would say to me, "I know a lot of people think I'm crazy with my angels, but that's what I do."

Mitzi (an appropriate name for a woman who's a bit ditsy at times), entered my therapy office due to anxiety and difficulty handling stress at work and home. Mitzi is an affable, chatty woman, who frequently misuses words. She might say, "My husband needs to go to Alcoholic Unanimous," or "you are a vast suppository of information."

Mitzi's malapropisms often cause me to inwardly chuckle during our sessions. But even though she may not find the right words, I always get her point. Mitzi's history suggests she has undiagnosed learning disabilities that made it next to impossible in the 1950s to get an appropriate education, so she dropped out of school in the ninth grade. Only within the last few years has she started reading books written for middle-school aged children. She is proud of herself for reading.

Mitzi married a man who was her first love, but soon found he was an alcoholic and womanizer. They had four children together and Mitzi entered therapy because after forty years of marriage she needed to talk about her miserable relationship. As with many clients, Mitzi decided she did not want a divorce for financial reasons but she wanted to find a way to be happy while living with this man.

Really, she thought ten years earlier he didn't have much time left on this earth due to his alcoholism, but he lingered, still sitting on the couch flipping channels.

Mitzi has always been the rock of her family—she is a grandmother who raised grandchildren, and now a great grandmother caring for her great granddaughter. Her love, compassion, and nurturing are a fundamental part of who she is to all people.

Mitzi worked as an aide at the local hospital in the pediatric wing. She loved her job working with the sick babies and their parents. However, Mitzi had a difficult boss who made her life miserable by critiquing every move she made, especially when Mitzi befriended the bereaved mothers of critically ill children.

Mitzi's obsession with angels began thirty years ago when she bought an angel for the parents of a child who died. This was the first death she experienced on her job and she was saddened for the parents. This angel meant a great deal to the parents and Mitzi remained friends with this family, visiting the child's grave every year and placing a new angel on the grave. Her angels have become legendary.

Often I find people who do these types of magnanimous acts, but all the while they look for acknowledgment and attention. Not so for Mitzi. She quietly places angels on graves and unassumingly gives her angels to grieving parents. What started with the preterm infants has expanded to people with cancer or victims of tragic deaths. Most recently she went to the gravesite of a murdered local police officer in the days following his burial. While she was there another police officer and his wife appeared and saw the angel. The police man was touched that someone would leave the angel for his fallen comrade. Mitzi just said, "This is what I do."

Now, Mitzi is struggling with radiation and chemotherapy herself, following a diagnosis of breast cancer. She is matter of fact about the possibility of death. Both her sisters died from breast cancer in their fifties. She says she wants to live, but if it is her time, then she's ready. She tells me the angels are out there waiting when her time comes, but she worries about who will carry on her tradition with the angels. I reassure her that the angels will continue somehow.

She wonders if after her death she will be the angel who visits. That may well be. I am sure Mitzi's compassion and caring will continue past her death.

Resources:
Songs about angels:
Angel: Sarah McLachlan
Calling All Angels: Train
If God Will Send His Angels: U2

Poem about angels:
Touched by an Angel, by Maya Angelou

Movies about angels:
Michael
City of Angels
Meet Joe Black

Books about Angels:

Jean Slatter, *Hiring the Heavens: A Practical Guide to Developing Working Relationships with the Spirits of Creation,* San Francisco: New World Library, 2005.

Doreen Virtue, *How to Hear Your Angels*, Carlsbad: Hay House, 2007.

James Van Praagh, *Talking to Heaven: a Medium's Message of Life After Death,* New York: Penguin, 1997.

James Van Praagh, *Reaching to Heaven: A Spiritual Journey Through Life and Death,* New York: Penguin, 1999.

Don Piper and Cecil Murphey, *90 Minutes in Heaven: A True Story of Death and Life,* Ada, MI: Baker Books, 2009

Colton Burpo, *Heaven is for Real,* Nashville: Thomas Nelson, 2011.

Chapter 43
A Mother's Common Sense And Humor
Patricia

SOMETIMES CLIENTS ENTER therapy to talk about one thing, but the session quickly becomes a discussion of many other components of their current and past lives. Such was the case with Connie, a peppy, cute, five feet two inch blond who came to see me with marital concerns. This soon turned into discussions about her mentally troubled son, which then became a conversation about her childhood and the loss of a dear father when she was nineteen years of age. But ultimately, my time with Connie was full of talk and laughter about her mother's wisdom.

When Connie first started therapy she was juggling a lot in her life: a mentally ill son, a husband who was distracted and distant, and an aging mother who needed to be moved closer to her. In addition, Connie worked forty to fifty hours a week in her new business as an interior decorator and house stager. As a stager Connie worked with realtors and home owners who were trying to sell their houses. Her job was to clean out clutter, organize, and put a fresh coat of paint on worn walls. It seemed to me that was also why she came to therapy—hoping to clean out the clutter and disorganization in her personal world.

As we worked on her marriage it became clear that Connie resented the role of primary bread winner because her husband had recently lost his job. She had always looked up to her husband and relied on him for financial security, and now he'd fallen off his pedestal and she was adjusting to a more human man. In fairly short order, Connie was able to appreciate her husband's strengths and sense of humor and realize his assets, even if that didn't include a big paycheck.

Connie's concerns for her young adult son were a continual source of tension. With the help of several mental health associates, a couples/family therapist, and a psychiatrist, we were able to form an accurate diagnostic picture of her son's mental health issues and come up with a future treatment plan.

Connie's decision to move her mom closer to her in an assisted living environment was a no brainer. When Connie was nineteen years old her father had a massive fatal heart attack in front of her on Mother's Day. Since then she'd always relied on her mother as a source of strength. Throughout our therapy Connie would whip out quips from her mom that sent me into laughter. She always was quoting her mom. She said her mom was her best friend, in addition to being a wonderful mother. Connie drew much inspiration and courage from her mother's humor and common sense. I share some of these thoughts with you to provide the guidance, wisdom, and humor of a delightful older woman.

Connie always spoke of her mom while using a Georgia southern accent. Her mother would say about finding her hometown: "You go to the center of Georgia and turn right; can't miss it."

Connie described her as a common sense, level headed mother who gave her and her older sister great confidence in themselves. She was supportive, but not overpowering. She was not an alarmist or worry wart. She was fun and wanted them to have fun. If Connie wanted to stay home from school sick, she had to stay in bed. "If you can't go to school where you can sit up and learn, then you can sit up in bed and read." There was a Southern saying of being "sick abed on two chairs," which meant someone was pretending to be ill or is slightly unwell. The idea is, you're slightly out of sorts, not enough to make you take to your bed, but enough to make you want to sit in a chair with your feet up on another chair. I guess Connie had to be sicker than "sick abed on two chairs." Connie said she only missed three days of school in twelve years.

Connie's mother was always fair. Connie said, "If I complained of a teacher being mean, her question back to me was, 'Why would someone wake up in the morning to be mean to you? What did you do?' She said there are two sides to every story. She didn't take my side unless it was logical to do so."

When Connie's mom was diagnosed with stage four melanoma in 1989, she refused chemotherapy and said, "I'll drink more water and flush it out of my system," and she did.

She said "I've had a bad hair day all my life and I'm not going to lose my hair over that." She died in 2012 at the age of ninety-two. She said when she turned ninety-two, "I've had ninety-two years of bad hair days!"

She was a fabulous grandmother and never added to worries by being an alarmist. She would say, "Don't worry baby, he won't go to college in diapers," or "She won't use a pacifier in grade school." Connie said this put a humorous, positive spin on childhood stages and worries. When her fourth grandchild asked if Grandma could sleep with him, her mother joked, "Yes! I don't get that offer very much."

After losing her husband, Connie's mom tried to make her daughters' lives as normal as possible. She didn't want to dwell on being lonely and as a result they always wanted her with them. She would say, "It was a gift that I had thirty-five years. I was happily married for thirty-five years; lots of people don't have that." Her advice on marriage was to not swear at each other, because "you can't take back those words."

"Always go out on Saturday night, because he is your husband and he needs his wife." She would say, "All kids want is for their parents to be happily married and not to worry about them."

"My father adored my Mom," Connie would say. "He would arrive home from work and kiss her first. I remember the warm feeling that they loved each other so much. The fact that he kissed us after her never made me feel I wasn't great. Didn't cross my mind."

Connie added, "There were no guilt trips about us going away on a vacation or having a party without her. My mom would say, 'I'm fine. I'm happy with my own company!'"

Connie remembers her mother encouraging her to go on vacation with her husband when she was still nursing her baby girl. Her mother said, "I can take care of her needs, but I can't take care of his. If you don't make it a big deal (about the bottle), she won't." Sure enough, when Connie returned from the trip, her baby went right back to breast feeding.

Connie loved that her mom went to Weight Watchers for thirty years, never quite reaching where she wanted to be, but always trying. She would joke, "I found the same pound that I lost." She was practical about food with a famous line, "That won't kill you" regarding expiration dates on food like yogurt. "Take what you can eat and don't waste" were her practical words regarding food.

Connie said they were taught to shut off lights, not leave the water running, and to "save money for a rainy day." Connie said she never felt poor, but learned to value hard earned money. Her Mom would say, "Keep your check book up to date. Make your bed. Have some order to your life and your life will stay in order."

These are sound words of advice from a wise woman. And it never hurts to keep a sense of humor.

Chapter 44
Embracing Our Inner Wisdom: Being Our Own Teachers

Helene

WISE WOMEN, AKA, "therapists" come in all shapes and sizes, educational and socioeconomic backgrounds, colors, and religions. Words of wisdom can be buried in the mundane, the banal, and the profound.

To find our inner wisdom we must first trust it is there, and then look for it: Be open to gut feelings and hunches that may reflect an inner voice: an inner knowing. Do what that voice tells you and later consider what might have occurred had you not listened. Recall times in your life when you didn't listen to the voice.

When I was eighteen years old and three weeks from heading to college, my parents reluctantly let me drive the family car a considerable distance alone for the first time. I wanted to visit my best friend from high school who moved away. I was excited at the prospect, but carried a nagging fear in my stomach. Perhaps I was reflecting my overprotective parents, but more likely I knew the risky behavior my friend was known for. On Saturday night she arranged a double date to a drive in movie, with me in the front passenger seat. My date got drunk and rear-ended the car in front of us, causing extensive damage and injuries. My elbow, which I had unconsciously thrown up to protect my face, went through the windshield. My friend was later diagnosed with a broken neck and went off to college wearing a cervical collar. I went off with a sling.

Anxiety over the accident and legal consequences fueled a depression two years later. How differently things would have been if I declined my friend's invitation to visit. I have used this experience several times as a "teachable moment" with my children and learned the deepest respect for gut feelings.

Have you ever had a terrible feeling, knowing in your heart a friend or family member is making a dangerous or ill-advised decision? We need to learn how to express these concerns without alienating others.

As a therapist I have listened to many people in the throes of new love extol the qualities of a new relationship, often with the phrase, "I feel like I've known him forever." I worry that this rapid involvement will end in heartache—and it often does. All I can do is identify red flags for my clients as they pop up.

Women with a history of trauma and abuse may have difficulty identifying their inner knowing. When a child never has the opportunity to feel safe and trust that a parent will protect them, the inner knowing may be distorted into self-defeating behavior, paranoia, poor judgment, and many other behaviors that feed the depression and anxiety that get people into therapy. On more than one occasion I've treated mothers who were victims of severe sexual abuse and felt very protective of their children, but would still blindly place them in the same dangerous situations that led to the mother's own abuse. The distrust trauma survivors feel makes establishing a therapeutic relationship difficult. How wonderful when these same people learn to trust their own inner knowing.

My wise daughter has said, "When it feels like too many obstacles are in the way of a goal, it's time for a new path." She is listening to her inner wisdom.

IN CLOSING

THE MOST BEAUTIFUL people we have known are those who have known defeat, known suffering, known struggle, known loss, and have found their way out of the depths.

These persons have an appreciation, a sensitivity, and an understanding of life that fills them with compassion, gentleness, and a deep loving concern. Beautiful people do not just happen.[31]

The Open Door,

by Danna Faulds (with permission)

A door opens. Maybe I've
been standing here shuffling
my weight from foot to foot
for decades, or maybe I only
knocked once. In truth, it
doesn't matter. A door opens
and I walk through without a
backward glance. This is it,
then, one moment of truth in
a lifetime of truth; a choice
made, a path taken, the
gravitational pull of Spirit
too compelling to ignore any
longer. I am received by
something far too vast to see.
It has roots in antiquity but
speaks clearly in the present
tense. "Be," the vastness says.

---

31   Kubler-Ross, Elisabeth, *Death, The Final Stage of Growth*, New York: Scribner, 1997.

"Be without adverbs, descriptors
or qualities. Be so alive that
awareness bares itself
uncloaked and unadorned.
Then, go forth to give what you
alone can give, awake to love
and suffering, unburdened by
the weight of expectations.
Go forth to see and be seen,
blossoming, always blossoming
into your magnificence.[32]"

---

32   Faulds, Donna, *From Root to Bloom: Yoga Poems and Other Writings,* Greenville, VA: Peaceable Kingdom Books, 2006, p.32.

AFTERWORD
WISDOM OF WOMEN

WHAT IS SO SPECIAL about women's wisdom, you may ask, and what exactly IS wisdom—and how do we develop it? These are questions we addressed as we imagined this book. For starters, we are living in an age consumed by violence that is more focused on consumerism and competition than the nurturing, peacemaking, and the healing qualities associated with women. We feel it is a time to refocus if our society is to survive.

From time immemorial women have imparted wisdom, whether around the campfire, around the dinner table, or over a glass of wine with friends. Wisdom can be found in unlikely places, including in the therapist's office from the patient.

Despite the fact that wise women have always been part of our world, we find scant reference to them in history books. In some societies, references to these important women have been eradicated and their reputations defamed. For example, did you know that printing the written word got its start in China, 700 years before printing reached Europe, because of a Chinese woman named Wu Zetian? We sure didn't, but Bettany Hughes in her fabulous article in the *Guardian* newspaper in London, "The wisdom of women written out of history," wrote about how China eradicated any mention of Wu Zetian.

She also spoke of Theodora, empress of Byzantium and wife to Justinian, who greatly influenced a code of law that is the basis of modern law. She is not normally given credit for that accomplishment, but is quickly identified as a former prostitute.[33]

Another famous "prostitute" is Mary Magdalene, now recognized by many as an influential friend to Jesus. In *The Gospel of Mary*, Mary Magdalene's sacred

---

33   Hughes, Bettany, "The wisdom of women written out of history," *The Guardian*, April 10, 2010, accessed 7/12/2012.

relationship is explored and jealous male early followers of Jesus are identified as her discreditors.[34]

Our patriarchal academic society has dominated the Western university system. That and male dominated Western religions have diminished the influence of women's wisdom. Jeanne Achterberg in *Women as Healers*[35] points out "that early women were often forbidden to speak or write in Latin, the language of scholars and the professions."

Two wonderful, interesting books to read to learn more about earlier treatment of women and their education are John Demos's *The Unredeemed Captive*,[36] the story of the Deerfield (Massachusetts) Massacre in 1704 and captive Eunice Williams, and *Caleb's Crossing*[37] by Geraldine Brooks, an historical novel depicting the first native American who graduated from Harvard in 1665. Most affecting in the latter work is the portrayal of Bethia Mayfield, the narrator and Caleb's friend, the extraordinarily bright daughter of Caleb's sponsor. She was relegated to a servant role, having to position herself carefully to try and overhear the lessons, since women were denied advanced education. It is suspected that seven year old captive Eunice eventually chose to stay with her adopted Mohawk community and marry and give birth to future chiefs because of the fairer treatment of women in that matrilineal society. Women were respected and had an important role in the tribe. These ancient people appreciated the power of stories and story telling. Husbands and wives were expected to respect and honor one another, and to care for one another with honesty and kindness—**women were honored for their wisdom and vision.**

I don't know about you, but it makes me sad to read the above description when I think of how some men and women treat one another with disrespect and the way entire societies systematically subjugate girls and women and deny them basic human rights, including education. If ancient cultures were capable of such respect, cooperation, and tolerance, what is wrong with humanity today?

So how do we become wiser to help us deal with all these societal problems? Well, let's first describe a wise person: "exceptionally mature, integrated, satisfied with life, able to make decisions in difficult and uncertain life matters, and capable of dealing with any crisis and obstacle they encounter."[38] Monika Ardelt, a leading

---

34   Ford-Grabowsky, Mary, *Sacred Voices: Essential Women's Wisdom through the Ages* (San Fransisco: HarperSanFrancisco, 2002) 25.

---

35   Achterberg, Jeanne, *Women as Healers* (Boston: Shambhala Publications, 1990), 2.

---

36   Demos, John, *The Unredeemed Captive* (New York: Vintage, 1994).

---

37   Brooks, Geraldine, *Caleb's Crossing* (New York: Viking Adult, 2011).

---

38   Ardelt, Monica, "How wise people cope with crises and obstacles in life," *ReVision* (Summer 2005) 7-8.

wisdom theorist and researcher, believes the process of dealing successfully with the problems and struggles of living helps us develop wisdom. She considers wisdom "a combination of personality qualities that cannot exist independently of individuals." She has identified three personality characteristics of wise people: the intellectual capacity to understand and learn; self-awareness and insight; and the ability to be sympathetic and compassionate. Developing these characteristics enhances our ability to address life's problems and learn from them.

One of the most profound and inclusive collections of women's wisdom is found in *Sacred Voices: Essential Women's Wisdom through the Ages*[39] by Professor Mary Ford-Grabowsky. When Professor Ford-Grabowsky realized that for years she had been collecting examples of the "Divine Masculine"—quotes from men's sacred voices from all over the world, she became determined to ferret out the sacred wisdom of women. She states, "Why was I ignoring not only other women's voices but the Divine Feminine in myself? I felt I was missing half my soul."

During the past thirty years, women's literature and studies have reflected the modern women's movement and helped us recapture the divine feminine. In *Goddesses in Older Women*[40] Jean Shinoda Bolen identifies influences on the third stage of a woman's life. She calls the first stage "Maiden," the second, "Mother," and the third "Crone." (The term "crone" is not a personal favorite of ours). Bolen feels this third trimester is a time of wholeness and integration; when what you do is an expression of who you deeply are.

We, the authors, Patricia Martin and Helene Houston, are in this third stage and feel compelled to offer the wisdom of our lives and the wisdom shared in the sacred spaces of our offices. Please find your own wisdom, from reading, sharing stories, joining a group such as Women of Wisdom, developing your spirituality, finding a cause, and working to change our society one precious woman at a time.

---

39   Ford-Grabowsky, Mary, *Sacred Voices: Essential Women's Wisdom through the Ages* (San Fransisco: HarperSanFransisco, 2002) 2.

---

40   Bolen, Jean Shinoda, *Goddesses in Older Women: Archtypes in Women over Fifty*, (New York: HarperCollins, 2002) 77

Our Stories

Patricia's Story

TWO WOMEN IN my life have had a profound effect on my major life choices. They are my mother and my paternal grandmother. My mother instilled in me the values of nurturing and common sense. My grandmother taught me about pursuing a career while raising a family. As a young child I was encouraged to be a good student and develop my God given talents. I have two older brothers and a younger sister and brother, making me the middle child and oldest daughter. This is an interesting birth order: both a leader (the oldest sister) and a mediator (the middle child). This birth order probably had something to do with pursuing a Ph.D. in the field of clinical psychology, a demanding and rigorous field, yet also supportive and other-oriented.

As a young woman growing up in the 1960s I came of age in the era of women's liberation; with women seeking equality in work, politics, family, and society. By contrast, I was raised in a traditional family of the 1950s, where my mother was a homemaker raising five children and caring for household duties, while my Dad was the bread winner going to work every day. In those days it was uncommon to know a mother who worked outside the home while raising her children. It was also uncommon to know divorced parents.

During that era female colleges focused on graduating teachers, nurses, or secretaries. When I started college in 1972 it was the beginning of coed education at many traditionally all male private colleges. I was encouraged by both my parents to pursue whatever academic goals I could attain. This advice was in marked contrast to my guidance counselor who said I should go to college so I would be an educated mother for my children. What? That didn't make sense to me even when I was only 16 years old. Would my quest for learning die once I had children? Would I never be able to have a career of my own? This did not jibe with how I perceived myself and who I wanted to become.

Fortunately my family was more encouraging. My mother, who did not have the opportunity to go to college, confided in me that she had always wanted to be a nurse, but due to finances and a lack of parental guidance she went to work as a telephone operator at a big insurance company. And perhaps fate took a hand, because that's where she met my father, a young actuary, and they lived a happy, loving marriage of 62 years, with five children, fourteen grandchildren, and nine great-grandchildren.

Another strong force in my motivation to succeed came from my paternal grandmother, Lillian Ford Peters, who was born in 1887. She was a remarkable woman who left home at eighteen at the turn of the twentieth century to find her fortune in Atlantic City. She opened her own beauty salon where she provided services to the celebrities of that era who came to the sea shore for vacations. She purchased several hotels and boarding houses on the boardwalk and became a successful business woman. She married at thirty-seven and had her first child at age thirty-eight, and her sixth biological child at age forty-eight. She adopted two other children who were orphaned in early childhood. When her youngest was ten years of age she was widowed and never remarried. Although my grandmother never had a chance to earn a college degree, she valued education second only to faith and family. I believe if she was raised in this era she would have graduated from college, probably with a master's degree in business administration.

All eight of my grandmother's children graduated from college, many with advanced degrees. As a teenager I would visit my grandmother during the summer, and she inspired me with stories of growing up as a young woman at the turn of the century. It wasn't until she was thirty-three years of age in 1920 that women gained the right to vote, let alone have careers and educational opportunities.

She encouraged me to continue my schooling and when I graduated from Georgetown University she was in the auditorium to cheer me on. She was eighty-nine years young at the time. It is largely because of her that I had the drive and determination to continue my studies and obtain my Ph.D. in clinical psychology. She attended my marriage in 1979 and died in 1980 the same week I discovered I was pregnant with our oldest child, who received my grandmother's name (Lillian) as her middle name.

My grandmother showed me it was possible to be a career woman while still being a loving wife and mother. My chosen profession of clinical psychology has been a wonderful way to balance home and work. I feel blessed to have a career where I enjoy going to work every day. I absolutely love meeting the interesting, resilient clients who enter my office. I have learned so much from them about surviving life's challenges and staying the course in spite of obstacles. I often leave my office in awe of the wonderful people I've been privileged to counsel in therapy.

Another blessing in my life is being married to a kind, good-natured man, who has been a co-parenting partner throughout our marriage. He supported my need to work and has been one of my most vocal advocates when working mothers are criticized. With flexibility at work and a supportive spouse, it is possible to successfully balance a career and parenthood.

As I write this book now that my four grown children are off creating their own lives, I think about how fortunate I was to have a mother who taught me all I needed to know about nurturing and home making, along with a grandmother who was a trailblazer in the early 1900s. Now I am reaping the rewards of being a grandmother myself, one of the most extraordinary experiences of my life. Another little love has followed my granddaughter, an active, sweet grandson, and another is on the way. The love of family, the love of a partner, the love of work: how fortunate am I.

Helene's Story

I WAS BORN LOVING school. When my older sister went off to school, I would play with my "little people" which included a complete old fashioned classroom, complete with inkwells. (I never used the inkwells when I was in school; I'm not THAT old!) I hope I instilled the love of school in my two wonderful daughters. I still miss them every September when the air changes and pencil boxes beg to be filled.

Being the youngest child, I spent a lot of time with my mother who also loved school. Sadly, illness prevented her from completing her goal of becoming a nurse at Columbia-Presbyterian School of Nursing. I loved my mother very much and always wanted to please and not disappoint her. Therefore, it isn't strange that my educational goals mirrored hers. Without any real idea about what nurses did, except for my mother's idealized memories, I decided to pursue baccalaureate nursing. In those days, choices were limited for girls. Nursing, teaching, and secretarial work were the most popular tracks. Thinking back, I loved science, so nursing wasn't an unusual choice. I also enjoyed English and writing and was rather put off when my senior English teacher at Ridgewood High School in New Jersey asked why I would choose to fling bedpans. Ouch!

I spent my first year of college at the Duke University School of Nursing which afforded a great social education, but brought up questions about my career choice. Duke was emphasizing the blossoming field of nursing theory which I found tedious. So, how does a young coed deal with career confusion? Transfer! I caught the transfer bug from other disgruntled students and arranged to continue my studies at Columbia-Presbyterian School of Nursing. Needless to say, my mother was delighted and post haste began volunteering at the hospital. Shortly after I settled into the monastic dorm room in the Washington Heights area of Manhattan, depression set in. Countless sleepless nights accompanied the worry of what a mistake I had made. The nursing program was heavy on clinical skills (which I thought I wanted) and light on respect for students. In 1965, Columbia-Presbyterian still had the feeling of male and physician dominance with nurses (and nursing students in particular) treated like second class citizens and handmaidens. Nurses still stood up as a sign of respect when attending physicians entered the nurses' station. Anyone who knows my personality would know how much I chafed under these conditions.

My favorite undergraduate courses, and the ones I excelled in, were the social sciences. Abnormal psychology was a special treat. I've always loved to figure out what makes people tick (perhaps to understand my own family!). So it makes sense that in my second year at Columbia, the classes I enjoyed and related to the most were the psych-sociology groups. These psychiatrist led groups encouraged discussions of the psychological and social issues of our medical patients as well as our reactions to what we were encountering. I experienced an epiphany during one meeting in which a short film was shown describing John Kennedy's Mental Health Act of 1963. The film included a description of out-patient mental health funding that would change the face of psychiatric care. Immediately, I realized I'd found my niche. Any thoughts of post-graduate work revolved around this goal.

I've been blessed to always love my work. I was also blessed to marry a man who would support and encourage my professional development. During the early years of our marriage few women in my circle of friends continued working after their children were born. Nursing has the advantage of offering shifts that accommodate family life. I have fond memories of feeding our older daughter and myself and having my husband rush home to continue childcare through the evening so I could do my shift. Looking back, the hustle and bustle of those times probably kept me from fully appreciating his sacrifices for me and the family.

My understanding of people and psychiatric treatment evolved over the years, starting with in-patient psychiatry, then as part of a crisis team. Earning my master's degree through Boston University School of Nursing (which sadly is no more) brought opportunities for more intensive out-patient work. In 1993, I obtained prescriptive authority and have been able to medicate patients as well as provide counseling. During my work I've been drawn to survivors of abuse and am in constant awe of their fortitude and resilience. Sadly, as I recall early cases when I worked on the in-patient unit, I recognize the signs of abuse and trauma we missed and the diagnoses that were labeled psychosis rather than dissociative disorder or PTSD.

I am so appreciative of all my patients who for over 46 years have shared their most personal stories with me and have been my teachers.

Book Club Discussion Questions for *The Other Couch*

1. Did your view of psychotherapy change after reading these stories?

2. Which stories spoke to you most about women's wisdom?

3. What do you think is the value of telling life stories?

4. Did one section of the book resonate with you more than another: relationships, loss, parenting, serious illness or other?

5. Two chapters discuss forgiveness: Chapter 1 and Chapter 8. What are your thoughts related to forgiveness in a relationship like the one portrayed in Chapter 1?

6. How did Chapters 19 and 20 about surviving the death of a husband affect you?

7. What advice would you give to Warrior Mom, Chapter 29, regarding telling her children about cancer? Do you agree or disagree with her decision to withhold this information?

8. What do you think of Chapter 6 on women's friendships? Do you often experience more closeness to your friends than to family members?

9. Did you relate to Connie's mother in Chapter 43? What are your memories of humor and wisdom from your own mother?

10. How do you think women's collective wisdom can benefit our world?

About the Authors

Patricia, on the left — Helene, on the right.

Patricia Peters Martin, Ph.D., is a Phi Beta Kappa graduate of Georgetown University and holds a doctorate in clinical psychology from Purdue University. Dr. Martin has done research work at National Institute of Mental Health studying bi-polar disorder and at the National Institute of Child Health and Human Development studying the effects of early environment on child development. She has taught and supervised graduate and undergraduate psychology students at Purdue University, Springfield College, and Bay Path University.

She has counseled thousands of people in her 35 years of clinical practice in New England and the Midwest. Her patient population includes children and families, individual adults, teenagers and couples. Dr. Martin also leads group psychotherapy with women who have been in abusive relationships. Dr. Martin has made numerous appearances as a commentator on the local affiliate of public television and as a guest columnist for a large metropolitan daily newspaper and its online affiliate. She has been married 36 years and is the mother of four children and grandmother of three. She lives in Western Massachusetts

Helene DeMontreux Houston, M.S., APRN, obtained degrees at Columbia and Boston Universities, and has practiced psychiatric nursing for 46 years in metropolitan Springfield, Massachusetts. While at Columbia University School of Nursing she was inducted into Sigma Theta Tau. She has provided counseling and medication management to thousands of people in a largely underserved population. She has spoken widely on the efficacy of psychotropic medication and been a guest commentator on the local public television affiliate. While at Baystate Medical Center, Helene taught medical students (Tufts University) and physician's assistant students (Springfield College) and participated in multiple continuing medical educational programs, seminars, and grand rounds.

In addition to psychopharmacology, Mrs. Houston has specialized in trauma work, mood disorders, codependency, and women's health. She has been married for 47 years and is the mother of two daughters and recently a first time grandmother. She lives in Western Massachusetts.

DEC 3 0 2016

CPSIA information can be obtained
at www.ICGtesting.com
Printed in the USA
LVOW04s0855231016
509929LV00009B/778/P